DATE DUE

~~JUN 20 1999~~		
ILL AVAIL 2496864		
10/29/00		
~~NOV 2 00~~		
MAY 29 2009		

DEMCO 38-297

The GOOD
The BAD &
The MAD

Weird People In American History

E. Randall Floyd

HH
HARBOR
HOUSE

AUGUSTA, GEORGIA

THE GOOD, THE BAD & THE MAD: Weird People in American History
By E. Randall Floyd
A Harbor House Book/March 1999

Harbor House
3010 Stratford Drive
Augusta, Georgia 30909
harborbook@aol.com

Book Design by Lydia Inglett

Library of Congress Catalog Card Number 98-75699
Publisher's Cataloging-in-Publication Data
Floyd, E. Randall, 1947-
The Good, the Bad & the Mad: Weird People in American History / E. Randall Floyd
First Edition
p. cm.
ISBN 1-891799-15-0
1. United States—Biography-Miscellanea
2. United States-History-Miscellanea
1. Title
920.073   98-75699
LCCN
Printed in the United States of America
10 9 8 7 6 5 4 3 2 1

*This one is for
Walter "Dutchy" Arntzen,
Eddie "Dukes" McCool,
the Goat Man,
and other strange travelers
I have met along the way.*

Contents

Introduction

*W*eird people have always fascinated me. As a kid I read everything I could get my hands on about Houdini and Poe and Lovecraft. Bela Lugosi and George "Superman" Reeves were two of my childhood heroes, despite their celebrated eccentricities and ignoble fates. In my teens I could not get enough of Edgar Cayce—the "Sleeping Prophet"—and "Bitter" Bierce, who gave us *The Devil's Dictionary* and *An Occurrence at Owl's Creek Bridge*. Voodoo queens like Marie Laveau haunted my dreams while carnival hucksters like P.T. Barnum held special appeal. Joshua Norton, the legendary "emperor of San Francisco," occupied a warm, fuzzy place in my heart. So did Lizzie Borden and Typhoid Mary and Nat Turner. I loved them all.

My boyhood favorite was the Goat Man, the old geezer who traveled the backroads of Dixie with a team of scruffy goats. Every few years he'd blow into town and enthrall wide-eyed youngsters with hair-raising tales about life on the open road. Years later I even got to interview him for the newspaper I worked for. It was one of the highlights of my life.

American history is full of weirdos. We know some of them—"Stonewall" Jackson, George Armstrong Custer, Nikola Tesla, Marcus Garvey, Cotton Mather. Others aren't so familiar—William Walker, Madame Blavatsky, Isadora Duncan, James McGready, Giacomo Beltrami and Colonel John Chivington, to name a few. All of them, famous and infamous alike, were movers and shakers in their own right and contributed greatly to the development of American civilization.

But all of them had one thing in common: They were weird.

Jackson, for example, believed he was possessed by demons.

Garvey felt he was the only man in the world suited to be king. Before he was lined up against a wall and shot, Walker billed himself the "gray-eyed man of destiny." Madame Blavatsky was in constant communion with the spirit world. In his quest to save souls, Cotton Mather, the great Puritan evangelist, sought to rid New England of witches. Nocturnal visions in a cornfield prompted Nat Turner to spark one of the bloodiest slave uprisings in American history. A Victorian beauty named Lizzie Borden took an axe and…well, everybody knows the rest.

Strange, unusual people have always been part of our historical and cultural heritage. But the history books don't tell us everything about these fascinating, notoriously naughty individuals. Some were saints and sinners, visionaries and villains, angels and assassins. Some rose to fame and fortune and led the country to greatness. Others lurked in the shadows, quietly orchestrating chaos and madness. All of them made history in profound, sometimes shocking ways.

The idea for this book originated years ago in a sleepy little village in Switzerland. At the time I was a young foreign correspondent on assignment. That assignment was to interview an obscure, thirty-nine-year-old hotel proprietor who had just shocked the world with an astonishing new book called *Chariot of the Gods*. My interview with Erich von Daeniken was a hit. Hundreds of newspapers around the world ran the story—compelling evidence, in my mind, that weirdness worked, that strange people made great copy.

That notion stayed with me down through the years. As my writing career careened from books and newspapers to film scripts and syndicated columns, I continued to seek out and write about strange, unusual people. While colleagues dutifully followed the antics of politicians and criminals, I zeroed in on Marie Laveau, Eddie "Dukes" McCool, the Goat Man, Tecumseh, Madame Blavatsky, Lizzie Borden.

Along the way I kept notes and collected biographical data. Tons of it. The result is this book, which I call *The Good, the Bad & the Mad: Weird People in American History*. By no means is this book intended to be an exhaustive study of each of the forty or so people profiled here. There are other books for that. Nor has it been my desire to exploit, ridicule, diminish or in any way portray these individuals in a particularly unflattering light. As my mother used to say, we are all flawed creatures and fall slightly short of the glory of God. Rather, the purpose of my book has been to go beyond the celebrated truths and often valuable contributions of each of these individuals, to probe their darker nature, to see what lurks on the other side.

In my dreams I can clearly see "Stonewall" Jackson, the tormented Confederate commander, sucking on a lemon while he charges into battle, arms raised high in an attempt to ward off demons. I can almost hear Cotton Mather's vaulted voice demanding confessions; Huey Long bellowing that "every man is a king, but no man wears a crown"; James McGready exhorting Kentucky backwoodsmen to get down on their knees and "shout out the devil."

These images remain, vivid and haunting, talismanic reminders that none of us is perfect, that we are all flawed beings. Generations of chroniclers have tried their best to brush aside these images, to rip them from the pages of history. But those images remain, drifting on midnight wings, disturbing our dreams of a perfect world, indelible hints that there is more to history than meets the eye. In a perfect world, Colonel John Chivington would not have charged at Sand Creek, William Simmons would not have climbed Stone Mountain, Ambrose Bierce would not have run away to Mexico. But we cannot change history and the deeds of our ancestors any more than we can control our dreams or divine the future world. The best we can do is to remember those deeds, to keep the good spirits alive and try to understand the rest.

That's what this book is all about.

E. RANDALL FLOYD
Augusta, Georgia 1999

Acknowledgements

$\mathcal{I}$ owe a debt of gratitude to many friends who have either read parts of the manuscript or provided information. These people include Duane Riner of the *Atlanta Journal-Constitution*, Lydia Inglett and Leslie Nelson as well as Liz and Ted Parkhurst who encouraged me to pursue this project. As always, a special word of thanks goes to my wife, Anne, who kept the faith and would not let me stray from the original concept. I also want to thank Uncle Curt, a mighty man and word warrior whose old black typewriter still crowds my dreams.

Jane Addams

The "most dangerous woman in America"

When she moved into the decaying old mansion at the corner of Polk and South Halsted streets, most of her friends and family thought she had lost her mind. Why, they wondered, would anyone—especially the daughter of one of the richest men in America—want to live in one of Chicago's worst slums?

But Jane Addams—beautiful, brilliant and bored—had her reasons. What the others didn't know, couldn't know, was that this pampered young socialite "born for a higher purpose" was secretly gearing up to launch a social revolution in the United States. That revolution would make her one of the most famous people in the world. In time she would become the darling of the masses and the princess of the media, earning praise from presidents and kings.

But that same driving desire to make the world a better place would eventually boomerang, transforming the young revolutionary into a "national disgrace" and eventually leading to accusations that she was the "most dangerous woman in America."

Today, some sixty years after her death, controversy still shrouds the monumental achievements of Jane Addams. Was she, as some critics charged, one of America's most notorious traitors, a contemptible radical who shamelessly embraced the Bolshevik doctrine while preaching international peace? Or, as others have put it, was she a genuine American heroine, a crusading martyr whose political activities and courageous stand against war, imperialism and social injustice helped her win the Nobel Prize for peace?

To understand this complex and controversial woman it is necessary to understand the world in which she lived. Born in Cedarville, Illinois, in 1860, Jane Addams grew up thinking God had put her on earth to serve a "higher purpose." Part of that belief stemmed from a childhood nightmare in which she dreamed she was the only remaining person in a world desolated by some disaster. Her responsibility in the dream was to rediscover the principle of the wheel.

The eighth of nine children, Jane Addams was a sickly child who had been born with a congenital spinal defect. She was hospitalized constantly and turned to writing as relief from her suffering. From her writings, it is clear that Jane Addams hated the corrupt, scandal-ridden world of her wealthy parents, a condition that worsened during the urban industrial horrors of the so-called Gilded Age. Especially painful to her was the miserable plight of the poor immigrants who flocked to the nation's cities in droves throughout the second half of the nineteenth century.

To this sensitive young woman, it didn't seem fair that so few had so much and so many had so little. (Her own father had made a fortune as a miller and local political leader who served for sixteen years as a state senator.) Thus, were laid the seeds of a bold new social experiment, an experiment that would culminate in the establishment of Hull House, regarded by many as the most successful "settlement house" in the country.

The idea for Hull House actually formed during a trip to Europe in 1888 shortly after she graduated from Rockford College where she studied medicine. While in London, she became interested in British settlement houses—places where the working poor could leave their children for instruction and care and where adults could come together for social and educational activities.

She returned to her native land, fired with a vision of improving the lot of America's urban poor, especially the immigrants. In Chicago, she would "rent a house in a part of the city where many primitive and actual needs are found, in which young women who had been given over too exclusively to study, might restore a balance of activity along traditional lines and learn something of life from life itself."

At the corner of Polk and South Halsted streets, she found what she was looking for—a dilapidated old building in the heart of the nineteenth ward. There, among the poorest people of Chicago's wretched slum, she founded Hull House in 1889.

Forsaking the comforts of her own home, Addams moved into the dreary mansion herself so she could "share the lives of the poor" and humanize the industrial city. "American ideals," she once complained, "crumbled under the overpowering poverty of the overcrowded city."

Soft-spoken and tenacious, the 29-year-old visionary became a kind of urban American saint in the eyes of her many admirers. The philosopher William James told her, "You utter instinctively the truth we others vainly seek."

At Hull House, transients received the very best instruction in a wide range of subjects, including English, Shakespeare, ethics, art history, cooking, sewing, music and manual skills. Working mothers had access to a day-care nursery and kindergarten, as well as a laundry, library, medical dispensary, employment bureau and art gallery.

Hull House was not the only American settlement house—just the most famous. In an astonishingly short time, its founder came to acquire a national reputation. As early as 1893 Jane Addams wrote to a friend: "I find I am considered the grandmother of social settlements."

Her continuing success made Jane Addams a person of considerable influence in Chicago as a spokeswoman for the foreign-born poor. Her books, including *The Spirit of Youth and the City Streets* (1909) and *Twenty Years at Hull House* (1910), an autobiography, spread the gospel of social work throughout the land.

"From the first it seemed understood that we were ready to perform the humblest neighborhood services," she wrote. "We were asked to wash newborn babies, and to prepare the dead for burial, to nurse the sick, and to mind the children."

Some critics considered settlement houses "mere devices to socialize the unruly poor by teaching them the punctilios of upper class propriety." But almost everyone appreciated their virtues, and by the turn of the century more than one hundred such houses were flourishing across the country.

Still, in spite of their apparent success, Jane Addams feared that settlement houses were fighting a losing battle. "Private beneficence," she wrote, "is totally inadequate to deal with the vast numbers of the city's disinherited."

True, slum areas continued to swell due to the annual influx of immigrants who came by the hundreds of thousands, mostly from the impoverished regions of eastern and southern Europe. Blighted areas grew more rapidly than intrepid settlement house workers could clean up the old ones.

"It became increasingly apparent that the wealth and authority of the state must be brought to bear in order to keep abreast of the problem," noted one worker.

Hoping to upgrade the shockingly filthy and overcrowded slums, Addams and her co-workers published systematic studies of city housing conditions and tirelessly pressured politicians to enforce sanitation regulations. To demonstrate her belief in direct engagement, Addams served as a garbage inspector for her immigrant ward. That meant rising at six every morning and accompanying the infuriated garbage men on their rounds to make sure every receptacle was emptied.

Addams often spoke of the "subjective necessity" of settlement houses. By this, she meant that they gave young educated women, whose professional opportunities were limited, a way to satisfy their powerful desire to connect with the real world.

"There is nothing after disease, indigence and guilt," she wrote, "so fatal to life itself as the want of a proper outlet for active faculties."

Settlement house work, she felt, was an attractive alternative for the growing number of educated women dissatisfied with the life choices presented them—early marriage or the traditional female professions of teaching, nursing and library work. Not only did it offer them a useful career but gave them a sense of purpose and personal worth.

The pioneering work of Addams blazed the trail that many women—and some men—later followed into careers in the new profession of social work.

But social work alone wasn't enough for this indefatigable young woman, who branched out into the women's suffrage and international peace movements. As chairwoman of the Women's International League for Peace and Freedom, Addams demanded that the United States not get involved in World War I.

It was this staunch commitment to peace that brought "America's sweetheart" crashing to earth. The once popular leader of social reform fell quickly from grace, assailed by her enemies as a Communist sympathizer and harbinger of Bolshevik revolution. Not a few super-patriotic Americans branded her "the most dangerous woman in America."

War came as a shock to Addams, as it did to many progressives, who saw it as an unnecessary solution to the world's problems. She responded by launching a vigorous campaign to urge women everywhere to pressure their governments into a negotiated peace. In 1915 she attended a meeting of the Women's International Peace Conference in Europe, then visited prime ministers to speak out against the war.

At home, she appealed directly to President Wilson. Unshaken in her pacifism, she stood firmly against the war, even after the United States entered the fray in 1917.

The clouds descended when Addams received a letter from a group of German women asking her to pressure President Wilson into allowing food to be shipped to "starving women and children." The State Department advised her to ignore the request, but when newspapers picked up the story they whined that "these are the same women who spit at our soldiers, who carry water to our wounded, only to pour it on the ground before their suffering eyes."

To many Americans, the letters, combined with Addams' renowned antiwar efforts and questionable links to activist groups, demonstrated that the famous founder of Hull House lacked patriotism. The old charges, however, soon gave way to new accusations that she was a Bolshevik and a dangerous radical.

In January 1919, Archibald Stevenson, a young New York lawyer working for the Military Intelligence Division of the War Department, testified before a senate subcommittee that he knew of sixty-two people who held "dangerous, destructive and anarchistic sentiments." Those persons, who had long been under government surveillance, included several well-known professors at major universities and many other liberals and pacifists.

At the top of the list was Jane Addams. Her name would appear frequently in a four-volume study of revolutionary radicalism published in 1920 and known as the *Lusk Report*. The *Lusk Report*, which became the bible of super-patriots, provided massive documentation for the alleged connections between peace organizations, women's groups and "all those who advocated social reform, with Socialism, Communism and Bolshevism."

Since Jane Addams' role in various peace and reform organizations was well documented, she was branded a Communist.

Throughout the early 1920s, as she continued to speak out against child labor and the Justice Department's raids on aliens and radicals, the attacks became more vicious and more irrational. "Reds Upheld by Jane Addams as Good Americans," screamed one newspaper headline. Another read: "Jane Addams Favors Reds."

One writer in the *Chicago Tribune* charged that "these radicals … are sworn enemies of our country and should be shot to death."

Even Hull House came under fire by super-patriots as a nest of subversive Communist activity. Through it all, Jane Addams denied any ties with subversive elements, stoically pretending the attacks on her character did not bother her.

"I have never taken these attacks very seriously," she wrote to a friend, "having learned during the war how ephemeral such matters are."

By the end of the decade the hysteria had passed, and the so-called Red Scare had waned. Jane Addams, the target of so much vitriolic criticism during the war years, once again came to be appreciated for her enormous talents and contributions to society.

At a testimonial dinner in her honor in 1927, Calvin Coolidge praised her patriotism, while New York Governor Alfred Smith declared, "In honoring Jane Addams, we honor the idealism of American womanhood."

On the same occasion, Charles Merriam of the University of Chicago called her "a statesman without a portfolio, a professor without a chair, and a guiding woman in a man-made world."

In 1931, four years before her death from inoperable cancer at the age of seventy-one, Jane Addams received the Nobel Prize for peace.

P.T. Barnum

Crown prince of humbug

In 1835, a small ad appeared in a New York newspaper announcing an amazing discovery—a forty-six-pound black woman who claimed to be the childhood nurse of George Washington, the first president of the United States.

Joice Heth, the startling ad proclaimed, "has arrived at the astonishing age of 161 years!" What interesting tales of "the boy Washington" the old woman could tell, the message went on, adding that anyone who doubted the story was invited to come see for himself "the original, authentic and indisputable documents" proving her identity.

In the weeks following the ad's appearance, some ten thousand curious New Yorkers trooped into the open-air Niblo Gardens to gaze upon the withered remains of a blind black crone who admitted under questioning that, yes, she remembered little George.

"What a naughty little rascal he was at times," chortled the old nanny.

Local papers buzzed with controversy over "the living mummy." At least one doctor verified the woman's age, adding that since she'd made it to 161 "she might be headed to immortality!"

Unknown to the press or public at the time, however, the writer of the ad and promoter of the event was none other than Phineas Taylor Barnum, the self-confessed purveyor of humbug, the fast-talking huckster who would go on to become the world's greatest nineteenth-century showman and impresario and later co-founder of the Barnum and Bailey Circus.

As local interest in the old woman waned, Barnum—then only twenty-five years old—took his oddity on the road. Everywhere he went, curiosity seekers ready to part with their cash flocked to his tent to catch a glimpse of the wizened "nursemaid to the father of our country." During a stopover in Boston, an anonymous letter appeared in the paper suggesting that Heth—whom Barnum had purchased as a slave for $500—might be a fraud.

"It's doubtful that she's even a human being," the letter writer pointed out. Instead, he suggested, she was a "curiously constructed automaton" of whalebone and India rubber.

Instead of discouraging visitors, however, the letter only served to whet new interest in the remarkable old woman. Exhibition halls soon overflowed with thousands of customers eager to see, touch and perhaps even talk to Joice Heth.

Not surprisingly, the anonymous letter was part of a carefully crafted publicity campaign orchestrated by P.T. Barnum himself. The scheme typified his lifelong belief that "every crowd has a silver lining." And in a career than spanned six decades, the self-styled prince of humbug would prove over and over again how easy it was to strip away the silver from a crowd and line his own pockets.

As demonstrated by the Joice Heth affair, Barnum, a deeply religious man who neither smoked nor drank, possessed a flair for showmanship that made him a world-renowned impresario. With equal ease, he could pass off a blind black slave as the nursemaid to George Washington or arrange a triumphant nationwide tour for Swedish soprano Jenny Lind.

According to biographer A.H. Saxon, P.T. Barnum was interested in three things—fame, fortune and entertaining the American public. While still in his teens, Barnum decided to accomplish all three goals by promoting "freak sideshows," a popular form of entertainment in his day. He felt no qualms about preying on the public's insatiable appetite for exposure to the weird and strange.

P.T. Barnum was born on July 5, 1810, on a farm in Bethel, Connecticut. His father died when he was fifteen, forcing young Barnum to work to help support his mother and four brothers and sisters. He first worked in a grocery store, then borrowed money to start a museum. The museum prospered, then burned to the ground. He borrowed again and acquired another museum, which also burned down.

But Barnum wouldn't give up. In 1835, at age twenty-five, he put together the Joice Heth scheme that helped establish him as an "American original, no-holds-barred showman." Such adventures and experiments would make him the most successful entertainer of the nineteenth century. It could be argued, in fact, that Barnum's controversial style set the stage for future generations of American entertainers, including modern talk show hosts Howard Stern and Rush Limbaugh.

On one occasion the unflappable showman proudly boasted that "the bigger the humbug, the better the people will like it." People, he said, liked being fooled, as long as they believed themselves in on the joke. The more whimsical the imposture, the greater its amusement value.

In 1841 Barnum purchased the American Museum in New York City for the princely sum of $12,000 and set about making it the most unusual museum in America. What was once a fairly traditional museum was transformed into a veritable freak show encased within permanent walls. The public eagerly thronged to Barnum's museum to view the strange things he had collected from around the world.

One of the biggest hits was the so-called "Feejee Mermaid"—an artfully concocted hybrid of monkey and fish. There was also a "woolly horse" supposedly found by Colonel John C. Fremont's expedition to the Far West, and a pair of Siamese twins (a term coined by Barnum) named Chang and Eng, who, amazingly enough, went on to father twenty-two children. The public's imagination was further titillated with such items as the Lucasis albino family; Ms. Jane Campbell, "the largest Mountain of Human Flesh ever seen in the form of a woman"; Mme Josephine Fortune Clofullia, the "Swiss Bearded Lady"; and "Zip," the cone-headed Negro.

Other star attractions included Admiral Dot, Commodore Nutt (all midgets), Jo-Jo the Dog-Faced Boy, living skeletons, fat ladies, a frog swallower, the Wild Men of Borneo (who, it turns out, were two retarded brothers named Davis from Ohio) and the Missing Link. No act seemed too freakish for Barnum, who parlayed his "international show of curiosities" into a sizable fortune while still in his early thirties.

Long before Barnum went into the circus business, in fact, he was already incredibly rich—richer, said some, than America's first millionaire, John Jacob Astor.

Barnum's prime attraction at the museum was a thirty-inch-tall midget dubbed "General Tom Thumb," whom he raised to world-class fame. The midget, a five-year-old boy from Bridgeport, Connecticut, named Charles Stratton, was billed as "a dwarf of eleven years of age, just arrived from England."

Barnum never apologized for his many exaggerated deceptions and contrived illusions. In his mind, he was giving the public what it wanted at a fair price. Whether people actually believed in the mysteries and wonders he presented was not his concern.

In his autobiography, Barnum wrote: "It was my monomania to make the museum the town wonder and the town talk."

By the mid-1840s he had done just that, amassing a personal fortune that made him a millionaire several times over.

But in 1855 disaster struck. A bad business deal in which he was swindled out of a fortune left Barnum on the edge of bankruptcy. To make matters worse, both Iranistan—his palatial Bridgeport estate—and his beloved American Museum burned to the ground. Instead of caving in to despair, however, the energetic showman rolled up his sleeves and went to work rebuilding his financial empire. A European lecture tour on "The Art of Getting Money" and "The Philosophy of Humbug" proved immensely profitable, and soon his museum rose from the ashes again.

When a second fire destroyed the museum in 1868, the irrepressible old showman decided he'd had enough. Instead of quitting, however, he organized a circus that, with characteristic modesty, he called "The Greatest Show on Earth." A decade later he combined the show with that of his chief rival, James Anthony Bailey, to form the Barnum and Bailey Circus.

In 1889 Barnum and Bailey took their three-ring act to London. There, two years before the great showman's death in 1891, Barnum enjoyed one of the highlights of his life—a standing ovation from an adoring crowd as he circled the ring in an open coach. He also met with Queen Victoria three times, as well as the King of France and royalty from other countries.

Barnum is perhaps best remembered as an exhibitor of "curiosities," but the people who worked for him—General Tom Thumb, the Bearded Lady and most of the others—loved him. He paid them well and took care of them. He even shared profits. He was so beloved, in fact, that when he faced bankruptcy in 1856, Tom Thumb wrote: "My dear Mr. Barnum, I understand your friends, and that means 'all creation,' intend to get up some benefits for your family. Now, my dear sir, just be good enough to remember that I belong to that mighty crowd, and I must have a finger (or at least a 'thumb') in that pie."

When Barnum died in 1891, a camera caught the Missing Link laying a wreath upon his bier.

Giacomo Beltrami

Dapper explorer was "doomed to wander"

The American West was a wild and woolly place, full of strange animals and strange people. One of the strangest men to wander into this untamed land was Giacomo Beltrami, a dapper Venetian dilettante and political outcast who saw himself as the world's last great romantic adventurer.

"I am doomed," he once lamented to friends, "to forever wander the earth on my pilgrimage."

In the early days of the nineteenth century, as he rambled the desert plains and lofty ranges of the high country with a pair of baggage-laden mules in tow, Beltrami cut an odd sight among disbelieving Indians who followed his progress with a mixture of amusement and awe. They thought he was crazy. Unlike other pale-skinned intruders who came into their midst sporting beards and buckskins and armed to the teeth with knives and guns, this frail, clean-shaven "pilgrim" preferred fancy clothing and never carried anything more lethal than a red silk umbrella.

Behind Beltrami's eccentricity was the unshakable belief that he, like Christopher Columbus, had a special purpose in life. While the admiral's destiny was to discover a new world, Beltrami's was to find the secret source of the Mississippi River. He never did, but after considerable hardship, he did discover a small lake, which he christened Julia after his beloved paramour.

The truly remarkable thing about Beltrami's "pilgrimage" through the American West was that he survived to write about it. Unarmed, unpopular, unable to skin a deer or even paddle a canoe, this blundering, hapless Italian adventurer, whom the Indians laughingly nicknamed "the man with the red umbrella," would later boast about his miserable experience in the American wilderness.

"It was absolutely indispensable for me to learn how to guide the canoe with the oar," he said after a pair of Chippewa guides deserted him in the wilds. Of the ordeal he said, "The fatigue I endured was extreme. ..."

Like legions of European adventurers who came before and after him, Beltrami went West to escape the stifling world of the Industrial Revolution. "Cast adrift" among the shifting desert sands and uncharted mountain ranges, the high-strung explorer hoped to make a name for himself and, at the same time, find a "haven in the wild," a refuge from an overcrowded world.

Beltrami's Pollyanna view of the West was common among European explorers of the day. It was an age of hopelessly romantic adventurers, most of them young and wealthy, proudly following in the footsteps of the great Prussian geographer Alexander von Humboldt.

Some sought adventure and excitement in remote, faraway places; others dreamed of fame and fortune in the fertile lands beyond the "shining mountains." All sincerely believed they had a divine mission to contribute something truly worthy to the world.

Beltrami's travels coincided with America's Manifest Destiny, a period characterized by a providentially inspired desire to move West and settle the new lands. Caught up in the energy of the movement, more than a few Europeans found themselves answering the West's siren call, either as noble adventurers out to conquer new worlds in the name of God or science, or as land-hungry speculators and settlers out to grab a piece of the wilderness.

In spite of the great dangers and frequent disappointments, these starry-eyed travelers blazed solitary trails across rolling prairie and remote mountains, pushed and poled their way down never-ending rivers toward unknown destinations.

They cleared land, fought Indians and followed the buffalo across America's heartland. In the process they became part of that great migration of peoples and ideas that flowed westward and helped shape the distinctive character of that region.

But Beltrami, with his haughty mannerisms, penchant for melodrama and quaint style of dress, was clearly not the stereotypical explorer-adventurer. Tall and aristocratic, the former Italian judge could be as testy as he was flamboyant, as reckless as he was anxious to help open up the continent's far-flung frontier.

In all ways, he seemed oddly out of place in the rough-hewn world of mountain men, buffalo hunters and buck-skinned Indian fighters.

Beltrami first sauntered into the pages of American history in 1823 when he teamed up with Major Lawrence Taliaferro, the famous Indian agent for the Minnesota Territory. Apparently, Beltrami had originally planned to journey down the Mississippi to Mexico but, for reasons now obscure, agreed to accompany Taliaferro on an expedition up the river to the Falls of St. Anthony, site of the present-day Twin Cities in Minnesota.

Perhaps he wished to view the mysterious Indian tribes whose "extraordinary character had, from infancy, excited my astonishment and incredulity."

In his mind, Beltrami had already connected the Cahokia Indian mounds near St. Louis with Mithraic temples and the pyramids of Giza.

At Fort St. Anthony (now Fort Snelling) Beltrami attached himself to Major Stephen H. Long's expedition assigned to survey the border between the United States and Canada. Long, a no-nonsense, scientific man of few words, disliked the arrangement from the start, but Beltrami tagged along anyway.

It didn't take long for the temperamentally incompatible pair to clash. Long described his eccentric Italian tag-along as an "amateur traveler," while Beltrami considered the major pompous and ill-mannered.

"Major Long did not cut a very noble figure," Beltrami later complained. "I foresaw all the disgusts and vexations I should have…to endure from litheness and jealousy."

Yet they kept together, forging steadily northward through thick forests and past smoky Indian villages until they reached Pembia on the Red River of the North, or "Bloody River," as Beltrami called it. It was there that Beltrami realized Long had taken him far north of the sources of the Mississippi, and, in a huff, struck out on his own.

Sometime later he hired two Chippewas and a cowardly interpreter to guide him south through country rumored to be filled with "ferocious savages."

This proved to be partly true, according to historian William H. Goetzman, who tracked the feisty Italian's journey westward in *New Lands, New Men: America and the Second Great Age of Discovery.*

"His small party was ambushed by Sioux," wrote Goetzman, "and the Chippewa as well as the interpreter ran off, leaving Beltrami sitting disconsolately alone in the forest gloom with his 'kit' and birch-bark canoe, which he had not the faintest idea how to operate."

At first, Beltrami fancied himself another Robinson Crusoe, deserted and alone. "But then," added Goetzman, "with visions of the intrepid heroes of Roman and Greek legend before him, he pushed on into the wilderness, towing the canoe with his supplies.

"Atop the supplies, like the Knight of La Mancha, he raised the boat's standard—his red silk umbrella—and struggled eastward through the rain and the swampy country of western Minnesota."

What kept him going was the hope—always the hope—of becoming the first European to discover the source of the Mississippi. To his way of thinking, Beltrami's quest was no less significant or noble than the search for the sources of the Nile, which was to attract a host of British explorers some years later.

He probably would have died in the wilderness had it not been for some Red Lake Chippewas who rescued him in the nick of time. They thought he was crazy, but ultimately guided him to his destination—the lake he named Julia after his lost paramour.

He saw—or thought he saw—streams flowing outward from the lake in two directions—one forming the course of the "Bloody River" and the other the source of the Mississippi.

Sitting on the shore of Lake Julia, Beltrami was overcome with elation. "Oh! What were the thoughts which passed through my mind at this most happy and brilliant moment of my life!" he wrote. "The shades of Marco Polo, of Columbus, of Americus Vespucius, of the Cabots, of Verazini [sic], of the Zenos…appeared present…at this high and solemn ceremony."

Beltrami eventually descended from the heights of glory and, after a series of other terrifying misadventures, reached Fort St. Anthony and civilization only to meet disdain.

"No one believed him," wrote Goetzman. "No one cared. The

source of the Mississippi River was clearly in American territory, and thus was diplomatically insignificant."

When he reached New Orleans, Beltrami published an account of his expedition in the form of letters to his beloved, the Countess Giulia Medici-Spada. The jaw-breaking title was *A Pilgrimage in Europe and America, Leading to the Discovery of the Sources of the Mississippi and the Bloody River, with a Description of the Whole Course of the Former, and of the Ohio.*

Ironically, Beltrami did not even discover the true sources of the Mississippi. That honor would befall Henry Rowe Schoolcraft, an Indian agent for the Minnesota Territory, who in 1832 found the waterway's true origins not in Lake Julia but in Lake Itasca.

But Beltrami's zany adventures and misadventures are not entirely without merit. During his travels, he assembled an impressive collection of Indian artifacts, many of which remain on display in Bergamo, Italy, his hometown.

And, fittingly, a county in Minnesota bears his name.

Ambrose Bierce

"Nobody will find my old bones"

"*I* am going to Mexico," Ambrose Bierce confided to a friend on December 16, 1913. "If you hear of my being stood up against a Mexican stone wall and shot to rags, please know that I think that's a pretty good way to depart this life. It beats old age, disease, or falling down cellar stairs."

With those immortal words, one of America's foremost journalists, authors and satirists disappeared into the Mexican wilds, never to be seen or heard from again.

The fate of Bierce remains one of the literary world's most enduring and fascinating mysteries. So many theories have cropped up over the years to account for the 71-year-old writer's strange disappearance they would probably fill a small library. Did he die at the hands of revolutionary bandits led by Pancho Villa as some scholars argue? Did he succumb to natural causes in the middle of the wilderness? Or, as others have suggested, did the celebrated misfit die quietly in his sleep in an insane asylum in California?

For years, newspaper reporters, detectives and secret service agents from the United States combed the rugged hinterlands of war-torn Mexico and Latin America for clues. Not a trace was ever found, leading one biographer to conclude that Bierce had "simply but stylishly" vanished from the face of the earth.

Whatever happened, it is highly unlikely that Bierce—whose gloomy, nihilistic works include *The Devil's Dictionary, In the Midst of Life, Fantastic Fables* and *Can Such Things Be?*—would have been flattered by all the hoopla surrounding his curious destiny. But interest in the Bierce legend soon reached international levels, eclipsing that of his books and columns. Everybody, from the queen of England to the president of the United States, wanted to know what had happened to the fussy old curmudgeon whose scathing attacks on society, religion, big business and government had flooded the pages of newspapers and magazines from San Francisco to London.

As Clifton Fadiman, the noted essayist, once remarked: "Bierce was never a great writer. He has painful faults of vulgarity and cheapness of imagination. But...his style, for one thing, will preserve him; and the purity of his misanthropy, too, will help to keep him alive."

Just who was this wildly eccentric iconoclast, this self-styled misanthrope and slayer of social conventions whom history bleakly remembers as "Bitter Bierce?"

Ambrose Gwinnett Bierce was born June 24, 1842, in Meigs County, Ohio, to Marcus Aurelius Bierce and Laura Sherwood Bierce, a poor but literary couple who instilled in their youngest child a deep love for books and writing. Naughty, rebellious, always masterminding devilish pranks, he left home at age fifteen to become a "printer's devil" at a small Ohio newspaper.

When the Civil War broke out in 1861, Bierce enlisted in the army and fought bravely on the side of the North—even though he sympathized with the aristocratic planter culture of the antebellum South. The young Ohioan survived the bloody conflict, but the war was to have a fateful influence on him for the rest of his life. According to biographer Roy Morris Jr., "Bierce discovered in the conflict a bitter confirmation of his darkest assumptions about man and his nature."

It was the war, said biographer Richard O'Conner, that unleashed the howling demons lurking in the pit of Bierce's soul. "War was the making of Bierce as a man and a writer," wrote O'Conner. From this grim experience Bierce would emerge—at age twenty-three—a young man with a true understanding of death, a destined writer "truly capable of transferring the bloody, headless bodies and boar-eater corpses of the battlefield onto paper."

Many scholars, including author Alan Gullett, argue that Bierce's war tales are considered by many to be the best writing on war, outranking his contemporary Stephen Crane (author of *The Red Badge of Courage*) and even Ernest Hemingway.

In a lifetime of writing and reporting, Ambrose Bierce turned out a nearly endless stream of short, razor-edged pieces of personal observations, collected in books with macabre-sounding titles like

The Fiend's Delight and *Cobwebs From an Empty Skull*. The books, aimed at exposing corruption in public life and the hypocrisy of life in general, won him a large following. Gloomy, morose, melancholy, sarcastic, bitter—these words have all been used to describe the man whom critics and colleagues alike dubbed "Bitter Bierce" because of his fierce, uncompromising literary assaults on what he considered a depraved and morally bankrupt society.

Profoundly disillusioned, Ambrose Bierce spent the next fifty years ridiculing and haranguing his fellow Americans about their own cherished ideals—be they romantic, religious, or political. He not only blasted government, big business, the military and "that old devil" progress but brotherhoods, fraternal orders and civic organizations of all stripes, reserving his sharpest barbs, however, for religion.

"Gentlemen," he once told a group of friends, "I maintain that missionaries constitute a perpetual menace to peace. The sons-of-bitches never give up. I know. My sister Almeda's somewhere in Africa saving souls. If mankind's lucky, she'll be boiled in a pot and eaten."

In 1871 he married—his first mistake, say some Bierce fans—then went to London to work as a correspondent. It was there that the stinging nature of his work emerged, along with his revealing nickname. Four years later he returned to San Francisco to resume writing. In 1896 he became a Washington correspondent for William Randolph Hearst's *San Francisco Examiner*, then switched to the *New York American* in 1897.

Never a happy man, Ambrose Bierce was haunted by dead ends, failures and tragedies in both his personal and professional life. In 1889 his son was killed in a shooting brawl over a girl. Two years later his wife left him, finally divorcing him in 1904. In 1901 his youngest son died of alcoholism. Finally, in 1913—old, asthmatic, weary, his creative power only an acrid memory—Bierce revisited the old places so dear to his memory: the battlefields of his "soldiering days," New Orleans, San Francisco, Washington and other cities where he had lived.

Then he went south—Texas—where, in San Antonio, he was given a dinner by his old army comrades. Afterward, he wandered along the border for several days before he finally crossed into revolution-torn Mexico. His last letter was sent from Chihuahua on December 26, 1913.

"To be a gringo in Mexico—ah, that is euthanasia!" he wrote his literary secretary before saddling up his horse and galloping away into the sunset.

Though never great, Bierce's writings were read, and after the events of his bizarre disappearance were made known, they soared to new heights of popularity. The stories, assembled in book-length collections, ranged from the supernatural and horror to the grotesquely humorous.

His acidic dislike for and lack of patience with the human race stains the pages of most of his writing, including his most famous short piece, *An Occurrence at Owl Creek Bridge*, which was made into a television film. Several full-length features were made on the Bierce story, including *Old Gringo*, starring Gregory Peck.

"Nobody will find my bones," Bierce wrote before setting off for Mexico, ostensibly to observe the revolution led by Generalisimo Francisco "Pancho" Villa. "I'm on my way to Mexico...I like the fighting...I want to see it."

As years passed, people on both sides of the Rio Grande speculated on his death. Did he commit suicide, as some experts claim? Was it natural causes, such as the asthma that had plagued him all his adult years, that ended the old literary warrior's life? Was he shot by Pancho Villa or some other renegade Mexican officer?

In 1923, his friend Adolphe de Castro went to Mexico to question Villa personally about Bierce. The old rebel told Castro that, yes, he had seen the gringo, but that he had ordered him to leave camp after the writer had uttered some indiscreet words in favor of Villa's enemy, Carranza. And what happened to him then? "Who knows?" the bandit replied with a shrug.

Another report that surfaced about the same time indicated that two of Pancho's hit men had, indeed, been sent after the aged American iconoclast.

Some investigators say Bierce didn't die in Mexico at all—that he made his way to England, or perhaps back to his old home in California. One writer even theorized that he spent his last years in an asylum for the insane in San Francisco.

Whatever the truth, Ambrose Bierce's curious fate remains as mystifying as was his own unfathomable life.

Madame Blavatsky

High Priestess of the Weird

*I*nto the shadowy world of Ouija boards, séances and ghostly rappings from beyond, there once sauntered a controversial character whose alleged mystical powers and outlandish theories on religion, the cosmos and lost civilizations shocked and entertained a generation of Americans.

Helene Petrovna Blavatsky, known to legions of devoted followers as Madame Blavatsky, was a guiding force behind the spiritual renaissance of the late 1870s that saw the reputations—and financial fortunes—of mediums and mystics surge to new heights of respectability.

At one point, this chain-smoking, hot-tempered daughter of Russian nobility and founder of the Theosophical Society would boast that she was more popular that either the king of England or the president of the United States.

In spite of her great popularity, however, there were those who insisted that Madame Blavatsky was nothing more than a fraud and a vulgar adventuress.

She once wrote: "I am repeatedly reminded of the fact that as a public character, as a woman who, instead of pursuing her womanly duties, sleeping with her husband, breeding children, wiping their noses, minding her kitchen and consoling herself with matrimonial assistants on the sly and behind her husband's back, I have chosen a path that has led me to notoriety and fame; and that therefore I had to expect all that befell me."

Born Helene Petrovna Hahn in czarist Russia, the future spiritual leader early showed a marked interest in fantasy and make-believe. One of her favorite childhood games was to entertain friends by telling them stories about invisible companions she called "hunchbacks." Her storytelling skills were said to be so great that she often frightened the other children and made them have nightmares.

When she was sixteen, Helene married Nikifor Blavatsky, a minor government official thirty years her senior. The marriage lasted only a few months, but she would style herself forever Madame Blavatsky.

While still in her teens, Madame Blavatsky—a tall, striking beauty with dark hair and exceptionally blue eyes—embarked on a series of global travels and adventures that would eventually take her to America. For the next twenty-five years, she wandered the world, visiting hidden monasteries in Tibet and the catacombs of Rome and Paris and studying the secrets of the Egyptian pyramids, eventually winding up in New York in June 1873.

Her timing couldn't have been better. Madame Blavatsky, now plump and graying, was immediately caught up in the wave of spiritualism and interest in occult phenomena sweeping the nation. At a séance in Vermont she met Colonel Henry S. Olcott, a newspaperman, lawyer and ardent spiritualist.

The pair teamed up to form an organization called the Theosophical Society, after the Greek words for "god" and "wisdom." The society's stated purpose was to investigate ancient mysteries, such as the secrets of the pyramids and the "nature of people of the distant past."

"A Theosophist," Madame Blavatsky once wrote, "is one who gives you a theory of God or the works of God, which has not revelation, but an inspiration of his own for its basis. In this view every great thinker and philosopher, especially every founder of a new religion, school of philosophy, or sect, is necessarily a Theosophist.

"Hence," she concluded, "Theosophy and Theosophists have existed ever since the first glimmering of nascent thought made man seek instinctively for the means of expressing his own independent opinions. Theosophy is…the archaic Wisdom-Religion, the esoteric doctrine once known in every ancient country having claims to civilization."

In 1875 Madame Blavatsky published her first book, an enormous and very confusing volume called *Isis Unveiled*. Critics snickered and were generally harsh in their reviews, but the massive work did succeed in gaining large numbers of occult-minded followers.

Highly successful, the book was followed by another in 1888 called *The Secret Doctrine*. In this landmark two-volume book, Madame Blavatsky reported that revelatory spirits from the Orient had taught her about the lost continents of Atlantis and Lemuria. Scholars and critics were quick to claim that much of the work was stolen from books by other occultists and crank scholars like Ignatius Loyola Donnelly's book on Atlantis.

Nevertheless, the book sold extremely well, earning Madame Blavatsky immortality among die-hard followers of mysticism and popular lost worlds' theories. Written in the same lofty, confusing style of her other works, *The Secret Doctrine* sets out the author's view that the Lemurians were the third of seven "root" races of mankind. The fourth race was the Atlanteans, who were said to have evolved from the Lemurians as Lemuria sank beneath the sea several thousand years ago.

Atlantis, which occupied a spur of ancient Lemuria, was destroyed about ten thousand years ago during a cataclysmic upheaval. Madame Blavatsky believed that refugees from that disaster escaped to Central Asia where they evolved into modern Hindus and Europeans. She also suggested that survivors might have fled to America, where they intermarried with Indians and gave them the technology to build the great monuments of Mexico and elsewhere.

It was in India while researching her book that Madame Blavatsky was introduced to the "Masters," or "Mahatmas." The Mahatmas supposedly were spirit forces that dwelled in the mysterious and remote mountains of Tibet. According to Madame Blavatsky, these kindly "lords of the unseen world" confided great secrets to her during their travels together—spectacular secrets about out-of-body travel, archaic history and the cosmic future of mankind.

Among the "fundamental truths" taught to her by the Mahatmas was reincarnation, the belief that "all people living on the planet are brothers immortal, living and reliving their lives."

By the late 1880s, Madame Blavatsky was at the pinnacle of her international fame and fortune. But fate was gearing up to deal her a crushing blow. A report written by famed English psychic investigator Richard Hodgson accused the great spiritual leader of being a fraud.

"For our part," Hodgson wrote, "we regard her neither as the mouthpiece of hidden seers, nor as a mere vulgar adventuress; we think that she has achieved a title to permanent remembrance as one of the most accomplished, ingenious and interesting imposters of history."

Even devout Theosophists began to regard their former leader with suspicion. Some questioned her stability, while others called her "a potentially dangerous woman." Growing numbers argued that Olcott should take her place as head of the organization.

Weary and frail, the once-powerful mystic agreed to step aside, then retired to a friend's house in London. On May 8, 1891, Madame Blavatsky died quietly in her sleep. The old Theosophist's body was cremated at Woking Crematorium in Surrey, England.

Lizzie Borden

"And when she saw what she had done..."

*F*all River, Massachusetts, was a quiet, remarkably ordinary little mill town tottering on the brink of obscurity until the morning of August 4, 1892. That's when one of the town's most upstanding citizens—a mousy, unmarried woman named Lizzie Andrew Borden—was arrested and thrown into jail for brutally murdering her father and stepmother with an axe.

By the time her trial was over, Lizzie Borden had become a household name across America. To some she was a demigoddess who should be hanged for her crime. To others, especially many in women's rights groups, she was an innocent "symbol of woman-hood" who stood falsely accused.

Also leaping to her defense were upper-class citizens and fellow churchgoers who found it difficult to believe one of their own could do such a thing.

Even though Lizzie Borden was eventually acquitted, she remained guilty in the minds of millions of Americans. After her sensational trial, which lasted thirteen days and attracted worldwide publicity, she went back to a quiet life of modest affluence in the same gray frame house on Second Street where the grisly murders had taken place.

By then, however, the damage to the former socialite and Sunday school teacher's spotless reputation had been wrought. The press, fueled by rabid public interest in the case, continued to run banner headlines focusing on the gory murder for years after the event, while crime writers and their publishers made fortunes telling and re-telling the story. It seemed that, guilty or not, Lizzie Borden's once proud name would forever be linked to the gruesome events of August 2, 1892.

The question remains, more than a century after the fact: Was she guilty? Or, as was suggested at the trial, did some unknown person slip into the house and slay the elderly parents while Lizzie ate pears upstairs and a servant woman worked in the kitchen less than twenty feet from one of the victims?

No motive for an outside murder has ever been clearly established, even though several robberies had been reported in the neighborhood in the days immediately prior to the crime. According to police reports, the Borden's house itself had been burglarized at least twice.

But because of several factors, Lizzie Borden remained the most likely suspect. At her trial, she gave a bewildering array of conflicting stories about her whereabouts during the murder. At first she said she was in the "backyard." Later, she said she was "in the loft getting a piece of iron for the sinkers." To another interrogator, she was in the barn eating pears.

More puzzling, however, was her neat appearance and calm composure when the police arrived. Surely, they reasoned, her clothes and hands and hair would have been splattered with the victims' blood. That is, if she were, in fact, guilty.

And the murder weapon? Where was the murder weapon?

A few days later an inspector rummaging through the Borden toolshed out back found a freshly cleaned axe head. Could this have been the cruel device that ended the lives of Abby and Andrew Borden? The fact that the wooden handle, from which it would have been difficult to remove bloodstains, was missing convinced investigators that this was, indeed, the weapon.

Then new evidence surfaced that further damaged Lizzie's defense. Upon request, she had turned over to police a spotlessly clean, fancy blue bengaline dress she swore she had worn on the day of the murders. That story seemed unlikely, however; no one wore party dresses of bengaline, a heavy corded cloth, around the house in the August heat.

Confounding the problem was testimony provided by a neighbor, Alice Russell, who reluctantly admitted she had seen Lizzie burn a blue cotton dress in the kitchen stove three days after the murders. The dress, Lizzie explained, had been soiled with brown paint—a color, noted the prosecutor, not unlike that of dried blood.

But an outraged press, supported by the public, rallied behind the frail, soft-spoken woman. Editors wanted to know how anyone could accuse "this innocent and loving daughter" of such heinous crimes without feeling ashamed? After all, this was the height of the late Victorian era, a time when the gentleness, physical frailty and docility of the well-bred American woman were cornerstones of society.

New Englanders were certain that well-brought-up Christian daughters like Lizzie Borden could not possibly commit murder with an axe on sunny summer mornings. Women possessed more "natural refinements," as one editorial put it, "diviner instincts" and stronger "spiritual sensibilities" than did men.

Overlooked in the public outcry against her arrest was the glaring fact that she stood to inherit a fortune of several hundred thousand dollars. Also, nobody pointed out that Lizzie and Abby had feuded frequently, mainly over matters involving Andrew Borden's money.

In the end, the jury returned with the only verdict possible under the circumstances—not guilty. The judge, who had admonished the jurymen to remember that such "a woman of refinement and gentle training…could not have conceived and executed so bloody a butchery," seemed genuinely pleased at the decision.

A few years before her death, Lizzie Borden moved to Maplecroft, the neighborhood she had begged her father to move the family to years before. In her final days, she undoubtedly had occasion to hear the nasty rhyme already being sung by schoolchildren to the tune of "Ta-Ra-Ra-Boom-De-Ay!"

> *Lizzie Borden took an axe*
> *And gave her mother forty whacks;*
> *When she saw what she had done,*
> *She gave her father forty-one.*

On June 1, 1927, she died at the age of sixty-six and was buried alongside her stepmother and father in Oak Grove Cemetery. But the public fascination with her case lived on, a favorite of crime writers, movie producers and directors, and even choreographers and playwrights. In 1965, an opera entitled *Lizzie Borden: A Family Tragedy in Three Acts* met favorable reviews. In 1980 *Blood*

Relations appeared, a play in which Lizzie kills for her parents' money, then dies after being found guilty.

In her own time, Lizzie Borden had become a *cause célèbre* of the women's movement and an example of Christian piety. Her acquittal was seen as a tribute to the American justice system and its main tenet of innocent until proven guilty.

But uncertainty remained. Quipped American wit Dorothy Parker: "I will believe till eternity, or possibly beyond it, that Lizzie Borden did it with her little hatchet, and whoever says she didn't commits the sin of sins, the violation of an idol."

Some skeptics pointed to Mr. Borden's bizarre relationship with his youngest daughter. "Daddy's little girl," as he called her, almost always got her way. When his mutilated corpse was found, Lizzie's graduation ring was still on his little finger. This happened several months after he beheaded all of Lizzie's pigeons in their barn—the same barn in which Lizzie supposedly ate pears while the murders took place.

Edgar Cayce

"America's Most Mysterious Man"

On the night of April 18, 1900, a young Kentucky photographer named Edgar Cayce suddenly lost his voice. His condition was diagnosed as "paralysis of the vocal organs," and it was doubtful he would ever speak again.

Unwilling to accept such a cruel fate, Cayce turned to hypnosis for relief. At the time, hypnosis was a relatively new branch of science, and very few doctors were trained in its application. Of those trained, fewer still were willing to use it.

But Cayce finally found a physician who agreed to take the chance. After ten months of hypnotic therapy, the twenty-three-year-old photographer's voice finally returned. It seemed a miracle at the time, but the truly amazing thing is what happened to him during those long hours of treatment each day.

Whenever he went into a trance, this shy, sensitive, deeply religious man who dropped out of school in the seventh grade, would talk about things far beyond his range of knowledge and expertise. In fact, he would often discuss complex medical matters, drawing upon principles, theories and terminology unknown outside the medical and scientific community.

In short time, Cayce was astounding the academic world with pinpoint diagnoses and recommended remedies for other patients, some of whom were hospitalized hundreds of miles away. Cayce was even credited with identifying and prescribing the treatment that eventually led to his own cure.

It didn't take long for news of this amazing "healer" to spread across the country. Newspapers and magazines were quick to pick up on the Cayce story, and soon banner headlines proclaimed him "America's Most Mysterious Man." One paper wrote, "Edgar Cayce Startles Medical Men With His Trances."

Cayce was startled by all the hoopla. Even more confounding, he couldn't remember any of the things he was credited with having said while under hypnosis! It was as if somebody else would step inside his body and speak for him, some highly trained doctor of medicine whose authoritative voice rumbled with confidence and wisdom as he spouted out prescriptions and remedies.

Gradually, Cayce came to appreciate his unusual mediumistic powers. Shortly after his remarkable recovery, he discovered that by lying down, thoroughly relaxing and taking a deep breath, he could duplicate the trances on his own. In such self-induced states, Cayce's voice would boom across the room, diagnosing problems and prescriptions for patients and visitors who flocked to him from all across the country.

There now had emerged two Cayces—a "waking" Cayce, the reclusive, soft-spoken photographer, and the "sleeping" Cayce, the psychic healer the media now called "the sleeping prophet."

Over the next several decades, Edgar Cayce would delight and astonish the world with his accurate and often reassuring predictions about future events. He talked about the past as well, especially the lost years of Jesus and prehistoric civilizations. In time his discussions ranged from comparative religions and dream interpretation to psychic and spiritual development, life after death and prophecy.

But most people came to his office for "healing" purposes— about fourteen thousand between 1901 and 1944. Copies of most of his readings are still on file in the archives of the Association for Research and Enlightenment, an institute set up at Virginia Beach, Virginia, to study Cayce's unique powers.

In all that time, there was never an indication that Cayce was conscious of a single word he uttered while in the self-imposed hypnotic state. Even though he couldn't account for this himself, Cayce theorized that the thousands of readings and predictions apparently came through or out of his unconscious mind.

Edgar Cayce was born on a farm near Hopkinsville, Kentucky, on March 18, 1877. Even as a child, Cayce displayed abilities that appeared to extend beyond the five senses. At age thirteen, for example, he had a vision of a lady who asked him what he most wanted in life.

"I want to be able to help people, especially children when

they are sick," he reportedly told the mysterious lady.

Shortly after his vision, Cayce found that he could absorb the contents of books simply by sleeping on them. That seemed to help him earn excellent grades, but he still dropped out of school in the seventh grade to go to work to help support his family.

In his late teens he became a salesman for a stationery company. That job faltered, however, when he came down with "laryngitis"— actually a throat cancer that reduced his voice to a bare whisper. The condition grew steadily worse, so he went to work in a photographic studio where he didn't have to use his voice as much.

Cayce turned to hypnotism when he realized that conventional medicine was not going to help him. Each time he lapsed into a sleep-like trance, the patient would babble on in his normal voice about complex medical evaluations, reincarnation, ancient civilizations, human consciousness and prophecy.

Several Kentucky physicians began using Edgar Cayce's talent to diagnose some of their most difficult cases. Cayce needed only the name and address of an individual anywhere in the world in order to give a detailed medical diagnosis and treatment.

By 1913, Cayce's fame as "the sleeping prophet" had reached international proportions. Hundreds of people visited his office each year, some from as far away as Europe and Asia. Each day he was flooded with requests for special readings that usually involved healing, although a few preferred "psychic readings." The telephone rang constantly, as did the doorbell.

Cayce, a self-taught preacher of the strictest integrity and character, rarely charged for his psychic services. But his conditions were strict: An appointment had to be set up for 11 a.m. or 3 p.m. on a specified day. The patient did not have to be present, but it was necessary that Cayce be given the person's real name and address—and where that individual would be at the specified time of reading.

Cayce's own routine never varied. He would usually come in from the garden or from fishing, loosen his tie, shoelaces, cuffs and belt, then lie on the couch. His hands would first be placed palms-up on his forehead, then across his abdomen. Drawing in deep gulps of air several times, he would close his eyes and relax. When his eyelids began to flutter, the actual reading would begin.

In the early 1920s, "the sleeping prophet" became obsessed with reincarnation. Often, when tracking patients' previous lives, Cayce would take them hundreds or thousands of years into the past. Occasionally, he would link them to the lost continent of Atlantis, where, he proclaimed, some of their "spiritual entities" had been born.

Some of Cayce's readings about Atlantis received special attention from the press. Not since Plato had anyone with so much authority spoken about the fabled kingdom that supposedly sank beneath the waves during a cataclysmic upheaval some twelve thousand years ago. According to Cayce, who frequently "visited" Atlantis during his trances, runaway technology was the cause of its demise.

In rambling, often confusing dialogue, he would speak of Atlantis: "In Atlantean land just after the second breaking up of the land owing to misapplication of divine laws upon those things of nature or of the earth; when there were eruptions from the second using of those influences that were for man's own development, yet becoming destructive forces to flesh when misapplied."

Before its destruction, Atlanteans had developed a kind of nuclear energy superior to modern-day technology. "Rays…invisible to the eye propelled vehicles through the air and beneath the sea," Cayce said.

Upon waking, Cayce was sometimes startled, even embarrassed by some of his pronouncements. A religious man who read the Bible every day, the last thing he wanted was for anybody to accuse him of being un-Christian. He was especially troubled about his comments on reincarnation, though day after day, reading after reading, his sleeping self always kept coming back to the subject.

Although Cayce's "life readings" on reincarnation and Atlantis deviated from his normal "healing" sessions, he would remain fascinated with those subjects for the rest of his life. In fact, Cayce's peculiar work in the field has been quoted numerous times by scientists, theologians, spiritualists and other investigators in the field of paranormal research.

Even more startling, one of Cayce's most famous revelations about Atlantis would come true, just as he had predicted in the 1940s. During one of his trances, he said that in the late 1960s, the western region of the long-submerged continent of Atlantis would begin to reappear near the Caribbean island of Bimini.

In 1968, just a few miles from Bimini, divers came across a group of undersea ruins that resembled collapsed buildings and some kind of ancient roadway system. Could this be the remains of the vanished Atlantean civilization?

Many followers of Edgar Cayce believe his most startling prophecy had come to pass.

In 1945, Cayce went to his grave, still bewildered by his strange powers and completely unaware of his unique contributions to the field of paranormal science.

Colonel John M. Chivington

The "Fighting Parson" of Colorado

The Reverend John M. Chivington came to Colorado in the summer of 1860 looking for glory. He found it four years later as the commander of a cavalry regiment whose mission was to "kill and destroy" all Indians in the region.

It happened early on the morning of November 29, 1864, when the "Fighting Parson" led a surprise charge against six hundred sleeping Cheyenne tribesmen camped along the lonely banks of Sand Creek in the southeastern corner of the territory. Less than two hours later, more than two hundred Indians, most of them women and children, lay dead or dying in the chill autumn air.

Chivington's action, celebrated at the time as a heroic achievement, is now regarded as one of the saddest episodes in American frontier history. The raid came to symbolize everything ugly about American-Indian relations and forced the government to reevaluate its official Indian policy.

Such a tragedy was bound to happen following the gold and silver rushes of the late 1850s when thousands of miners and settlers poured into the Colorado Territory, dislocating and infuriating the Indians who lived there. When bands of young warriors struck back in the early 1860s, raiding stagecoaches and wagon trains and setting frontier towns ablaze, the terrified citizens of Denver petitioned Territorial Governor John Evans for protection.

Evans, a conscientious and ambitious man whose vision of Colorado's "grand destiny" did not include Indians, responded by issuing a proclamation authorizing white citizens to "pursue…kill and destroy savages."

Apparently, the governor had forgotten that he and his military commanders in the region had previously promised to protect those same "savages" from the army and Colorado citizens.

Back in February 1861, in order to make room for white settlement expansion, federal commissioners at Fort Lyon had forced Cheyenne and Arapaho tribal leaders to abandon all claims to territory granted them earlier in the Fort Laramie Treaty. In exchange for those lands, the tribes would be granted a small reservation between the Arkansas River and Sand Creek in the eastern corner of the territory.

Many warriors refused to accept the council's ruling. Instead, they angrily denounced their own chiefs and took to the warpath. For the next three years they waged unrelenting warfare against mining camps, mail stations, emigrant trains and outlying towns. When Denver was threatened, its citizens demanded that Governor Evans send the army after the renegade Indians.

The responsibility for putting down the uprising rested squarely on the broad shoulders of big John Chivington, the arrogant, hot-headed territorial military commander who ruled his troopers with almost hypnotic powers. A former Civil War hero and Methodist minister with political ambitions of his own, Chivington jumped at the opportunity to make a name for himself in the Colorado wilds.

He had come to Colorado in 1860, sent by his church to establish the Rocky Mountain Conference. A roaring abolitionist, Chivington, it was rumored, often delivered sermons with a Bible in one hand and a cocked revolver in the other. On one occasion, while presiding over a Missouri congregation, he responded to threats from pro-slavery agitators by whipping out two pistols and proclaiming: "By the grace of God and these two revolvers, I am going to preach here today."

When the Civil War broke out, the governor of the Colorado Territory offered Chivington a commission as an army chaplain—an offer the "Fighting Parson" promptly turned down in favor of a "fighting" position. In 1862, Chivington, by that point a major in the first Colorado Volunteer Regiment, played a critical role in defeating Confederate forces at Glorietta Pass in eastern New Mexico, where his troops rappelled down canyon walls in a surprise attack on the enemy's supply train. He was widely hailed as a military hero.

Back in Denver after the defeat of the Confederacy's western forces, Chivington seemed destined for even greater prominence. He was a leading advocate of quick statehood for Colorado and the likely Republican candidate for the state's first congressional seat. In the midst of his blossoming political prospects, tensions between Colorado's burgeoning white population and the Cheyenne Indians reached a feverish pitch.

The Denver newspaper printed a front-page editorial advocating the "extermination of the red devils" and urging its readers to "take a few months off and dedicate that time to wiping out the Indians."

Although not technically at war with the Cheyenne, Chivington and Colorado Territory Governor Evans conspired in the spring of 1864 to go on the offensive. Prompted by Denver newspapers, Chivington hastily formed the Third Cavalry, basically a volunteer unit of about one thousand men, including a large number of rowdies and toughs recruited from mining camps and Denver saloons. Chivington's orders were to "burn villages and kill Cheyennes wherever and whenever found."

When someone protested Chivington's heavy-handed order, the colonel is said to have thundered, "I believe it to be right and honorable to use any means under God's heaven to kill Indians that would kill women and children, and damn any man that was in sympathy with Indians." He added: "The Cheyennes will have to be roundly whipped—or completely wiped out—before they will be quiet. I say that if any of them are caught in your vicinity, the only thing to do is kill them."

Caught up in the turmoil was an aging Cheyenne chief named Black Kettle. Gentle, wise, wrinkled by sixty Plains winters, Black Kettle believed peace with the white man was the only way to preserve his peoples' freedom to follow the buffalo. While the war spirit continued to fire some of the younger braves, Black Kettle preached cooperation with the whites, even if it meant yielding even more of the tribe's ancestral lands.

At the Fort Lyon council, Black Kettle had made clear his desire for peace, but the federal commander informed him that he did not have the authority to end the war. In late September, Black Kettle and other Cheyenne and Arapaho chiefs held a conference with

Governor Evans, who also refused to accept their overtures for peace and declared that the war would continue.

Echoing Evans' sentiment, Major General Samuel R. Curtiss proclaimed, "I want no peace till the Indians suffer more."

A month later, while addressing a gathering of church deacons, Chivington dismissed the possibility of making a treaty with the Cheyenne: "It simply is not possible for Indians to obey or even understand any treaty. I am fully satisfied, gentlemen, that to kill them is the only way we will ever have peace and quiet in Colorado."

For reasons still unclear, Black Kettle believed the war was over and led his followers to Sand Creek, where he hoped his people would be safe, far removed from the world of the white man and the fighting taking place there.

Through October and November, Colonel Chivington bore mounting abuse from the Colorado press, which ridiculed him and his newly formed cavalry unit for failing to take action against the Indians. He briefly considered leading an expedition against a group of hostile Sioux along the upper Republican River but decided that Black Kettle's band of Cheyenne and Arapahos at Sand Creek posed a much easier target.

So at daybreak on November 29, Chivington sent his soldiers charging into Black Kettle's sleeping camp. When he heard the troopers coming, Black Kettle hoisted first an American flag over his lodge, which indicated he was not at war with the United States, then a white flag. But the riders kept charging, swinging their sabers and blasting away with rifles, pistols and even a couple of howitzers brought from Fort Lyon.

Frantically, the dazed Cheyenne fled in all directions, seeking cover, as the thundering horsemen cut them down. They had no chance to organize any kind of resistance, and for several hours Chivington's men ranged the countryside in search of survivors, honoring their commander's orders that no prisoners be taken. Men, women, children and even infants perished in the orgy of slaughter, their bodies scalped and barbarously mutilated.

"Here was Indian war at its worst," commented one historian about the massacre. "Whites engaging in methods they had long condemned as uncivilized."

When the carnage ended, the village had been destroyed and about a fifth of its inhabitants murdered. Black Kettle and the remnants escaped into the hills. Only nine Colorado Volunteers had been lost in the hour-long battle.

The action near Fort Lyon has often been called the "Chivington Massacre" or the "Sand Creek Massacre." But most Coloradans, grateful to be free of Indian danger, termed it a punitive expedition and professed to be pleased with the results. When Chivington and his "Blood Thirsters" returned to Denver, thousands of cheering citizens turned out to welcome them back as conquering heroes. "Colorado soldiers have again covered themselves with glory," exulted the *Rocky Mountain News*, as the victors of Sand Creek paraded triumphantly throughout downtown areas.

Theater patrons applauded a garish display of Cheyenne scalps, some of them women's pubic hair, strung across the stage at intermission. When it was revealed that many children had been killed in the raid, most of Denver's white population agreed with Chivington's justification: "Nits make lice."

Only later did the grim truth about the massacre emerge. It came during testimony at three special congressional investigations into the actions of the "Fighting Parson" and his men at Sand Creek. While some of the participants in the massacre supported Chivington's actions, most were strongly critical.

Samuel G. Colley, an Indian agent, testified that "some of the chiefs did not lift an arm, but stood there and were shot down." Those who ran, he said, "were followed up and pursued and killed and butchered...in a brutal manner and scalped and mutilated as bad as an Indian ever did to a white man."

Smith added, "I saw the bodies of those lying there cut all to pieces, worse mutilated than any I ever saw before, the women cut all to pieces. They were cut with knives, scalped, their brains knocked out. Children two or three months old; all ages lying there, from sucking infants to warriors."

First Lieutenant James D. Cannon gave this account: "I did not see a body of man, woman or child but was scalped, and in many instances their bodies were mutilated in the most horrible manner—men, women and children's private parts cut out, etc.; I heard one man say that he had cut out a woman's private parts and had them for exhibition on a stick. ... I heard of one instance of a child a few months old being thrown in the feedbox of a wagon, and after being carried some distance left on the ground to perish.

"I also heard of numerous instances in which men had cut out the private parts of females and stretched them over the saddlebows, and wore them over their hats while riding in the ranks. ..."

A sergeant noted: "I think among the dead bodies one-third were women and children. The bodies were horribly cut up, skulls broken in a good many; I judge they were broken in after they were killed, as they were shot besides."

Some Coloradans felt that Chivington's Massacre, brutal though it was, had merely evened up the score for a number of past Indian crimes. Very shortly, more treaties were signed with the natives— Apache, Kiowa, Comanche, Arapaho and Cheyenne, in particular— and more land was ceded.

For the southern Cheyenne, however, their tragic fate was only beginning. In the days that followed, these unfortunate victims of Chivington's carnage would be forced to surrender the last vestiges of their land in exchange for new homes in Indian Territory, which would ultimately become the state of Oklahoma.

Although he was never punished for his role at Sand Creek, Chivington did at least pay some price. He was forced to resign from the Colorado militia, to withdraw from politics and to stay away from the campaign for statehood. In 1865, he moved to Nebraska, spending several unsuccessful years as a freight hauler. He lived briefly in California, then returned to Ohio, where he resumed farming and became editor of a small newspaper.

In 1883 he reentered politics with a campaign for a state legislature seat, but charges of his guilt in the Sand Creek massacre forced him to withdraw. He quickly returned to Denver and worked as a deputy sheriff until shortly before his death from cancer in 1892.

James Churchward

"Unimagined worlds, far beyond the horizon"

"The Garden of Eden was not in Asia but on a now sunken continent in the Pacific Ocean."

With that startling statement begins one of the strangest and most controversial books of the twentieth century, *The Lost Continent of Mu*, which first appeared in the late 1920s amid considerable scientific speculation about lost worlds and vanished civilizations. Its author, an elderly American archaeologist and mystic named James Churchward, claimed to have discovered the truth about Mu in documents found in a monastery in India.

Churchward's book, which became an instant bestseller and remains in print even today, was one of many such works seeking to prove through mystical revelations and pseudo-scientific research the existence of long-vanished kingdoms known to history as Atlantis, Lemuria, Prester John's Kingdom and Pan.

According to Churchward, who preferred the title of "Colonel," which he had earned while serving with the British Army, the Biblical story of creation came first not from the peoples of the Nile or the Euphrates Valley, but from the peoples of the submerged continent of Mu.

"The oldest records of man are not to be found in Egypt or the Valley of the Euphrates," he noted, "but right here in North America and in the Orient where Mu planted her first colonies."

This knowledge was revealed to the colonel in 1868 by an old Hindu priest who taught him an ancient language, Naacal, which Churchward believed was the original tongue of all mankind. From there, the archaeologist was able to decipher the story of Mu on ancient stone tablets hidden for centuries in the priest's temple.

The tablets revealed that man first appeared in Mu millions of years ago, at a time when dinosaurs walked the earth, and that a sophisticated race of sixty-four million people had somehow evolved. Unfortunately, this idyllic land rested on a foundation of gas-filled caves. During the last Ice Age—about twenty-five thousand years ago—this gas exploded in a great cataclysm, and Mu sank beneath the waves. But there were some survivors, and from them sprang all the world's present races.

"By comparing this writing with records of other ancient civilizations, as revealed in written documents, prehistoric ruins and geological phenomena," Churchward wrote, "I found that all these centers of civilization had drawn their culture from a common source—Mu."

The indefatigable archaeologist spent more than half a century studying the Naacal tablets along with 2,500 others discovered in Mexico. Both sets, he asserted, originated in the same place—"the motherland of Mu."

Exactly where was Mu located? According to Churchward, the lost continent had extended from somewhere north of Hawaii to the south as far as the Fijis and Easter Island. Such a location would account for white races in the South Sea Islands, he pointed out.

"I learned that in this beautiful country there had lived a people that colonized the earth, and that the land had been obliterated by terrific earthquakes and submersion 25,000 years ago and had vanished in a vortex of fire and water," he explained.

According to Churchward, the collection of tablets provides an enthralling portrait not only of the ancient motherland but of the creation and what he calls the "Four Great Cosmic Forces."

The tablets "indubitably establish to my own satisfaction that at one time the earth had an incalculably ancient civilization, which was, in many respects, superior to our own, and far in advance of us in some important essentials which the modern world is just beginning to have cognizance of," he wrote. "These tablets, with other ancient records, bear witness to the amazing fact that the civilizations of India, Babylonia, Persia, Egypt and Yucatán were but the dying embers of the first great civilization."

At its height, Mu was a highly civilized, peaceful kingdom populated with enlightened citizens. "There was no savagery on the face of the earth," he wrote, "nor had there ever been, since all the peoples on earth were children of Mu and under the suzerainty of the motherland."

Churchward described the original inhabitants of Mu as "exceedingly handsome people, with clear white or olive skins, large soft, dark eyes and straight black hair." Besides the dominant white race, he said there were others—"people with yellow, brown and black skins. They, however, did not dominate."

The ancient islanders, said Churchward, were great navigators and sailors who took their ships all over the world, "from the eastern to the western oceans and from the northern to the southern seas. ... They were also learned architects, building great temples and palaces of stone."

Then came that terrible night when the seas darkened and thunder shook the kingdom's tall, gleaming columns and the waves came crashing in over her "clean-washed streets and handsome houses."

It was over in less than an hour. Survivors clung to floating debris and the pointed tips of islands as their homeland sank lower and lower into the boiling abyss.

Where once laughing children romped beneath a tropical sun and crystal rivers flowed across flat, leafy meadows, there was nothing. Mu, the great motherland, was gone, swallowed up in the night.

Just how many people survived Churchward found impossible to determine. But by comparing certain cultural, linguistic, architectural and religious traditions that exist in the world today, the author concluded that one group of survivors sailed away to the east, settling in Asia, while a second wave made its way across the Pacific to North America.

He points to the Hopi and Zuni Pueblos in North America as proof that Indians are descended from ancestors who fled Mu.

"Their connection with the motherland is perfectly established," he explained. "Their traditions tell us that they originally came to America from Mu. All their religious inspirations are traceable back to the first religion of man, and their sacred symbols are virtually those of Mu."

As additional proof, he points to a legend of the Pueblos Indians that their forefathers came to America in ships from across the sea "in the direction of the setting sun."

"Thus," wrote Churchward, "it is shown that they came to America from the west, in ships, not over the much abused and imposed on Bering land bridge."

The last colonizers to reach America were the so-called Cliff Dwellers of the Four Corners region of Utah, Arizona, Colorado and New Mexico. Even their relatively late arrival preceded the raising of the mountains, Churchward maintained.

Of all the theories advanced in Churchward's book, none is more fascinating—or bewildering—than that of man's age on earth. According to Churchward, human beings were building cities and writing poetry long before the arrival of dinosaurs and the formation of modern mountain ranges.

Once again, he points to another Zuni myth as evidence. "The ancient Zunis, thousands upon thousands of years ago, had a perfect knowledge of the great reptilian monstrosities that frequented the earth from the Carboniferous Age down to the end of the Cretaceous Period. The traditions say: 'They were monsters and animals of prey; they were provided with claws and terrible teeth. A mountain lion is but a mole compared to them.' "

In spite of Churchward's monumental book, no other accounts have ever been found to substantiate his esoteric claims of a sunken Pacific continent. His Naacal tablets seem to have mysteriously disappeared, along with all evidence of his 1866 visit to an Indian monastery. So far, no geologist has discovered a subterranean world of crumbling white columns.

Yet, as with Atlantis and other tales of long-lost continents, Colonel Churchward's strange story continues to entertain and astound even today's staunchest skeptics.

"Wrong-Way" Corrigan

"Anybody can make an honest mistake"

*A*s a teenager growing up in post-World War I California, Douglas Corrigan was obsessed with the idea of owning his own airplane. His dream, one that followed him into early adulthood, was to someday fly that airplane across the Atlantic Ocean.

In the mid-1930s, part of Corrigan's dream finally came true when he scraped up enough money to buy himself a plane. It wasn't much—just an old wood-framed Curtiss Robin monoplane with a leaky cockpit and worn-out engine—but it was all the young aviation mechanic could afford at the time. Besides, he told friends and neighbors, he'd have the old heap fixed up and airworthy in no time.

While he worked on the plane, he continued to dream about that solo transatlantic flight. Sometimes he'd talk about those plans with others. "I'm gonna go, you just wait and see," he boasted, ignoring the sneers and jeers as he continued to patch up wings, repair the propeller, tighten up the flaps and replace landing gear.

When questioned about his lack of aviation experience, he'd point proudly to his years as an aviation mechanic. Not only did he know airplanes, he'd taught himself how to fly. He'd even worked on the *Spirit of St. Louis*, the airplane owned by his idol—world-famous aviator Charles Lindbergh, whose exciting, transatlantic solo flight to Paris had made him an international celebrity.

Lindbergh's success inspired Corrigan to duplicate the feat. He obtained his pilot's license in December 1927, and an air transport license three years later. He barnstormed for a few years, and, in 1933, for $325, bought the OX5 Robin that would eventually bring him fame.

By 1937 Corrigan was ready. He installed extra fuel tanks and overhauled his Robin. The only thing left to do was apply for permission from the United States Bureau of Air Commerce for clearance to fly the Atlantic. A mere formality, he mused—until his request was rejected.

The next summer, after having spent many months refitting the aircraft, Corrigan was given official permission to make a three-thousand-mile solo flight from Los Angeles to New York—but no more.

At last, Corrigan thought as he climbed into the cockpit of the dilapidated Robin to set forth on what would become one of the most incredible flights in aviation history.

Nobody believed it when the quaking plane, smoking and hissing, finally lifted off the runway in Los Angeles for the twelve-hour flight to New York. When the plane landed on time at Floyd Bennett Field in New York, everyone took it to be a miracle. Not only had crew and mechanics scurried out of the way when they stared in disbelief at the ragged old heap approaching them, some apprehensive workers threatened to quit and leave town if the amateurish pilot was allowed to take off again.

A couple of days later he was given permission to take off anyway, in spite of a light fog. Officials in the control tower and on the ground watched terror-stricken as the shuddering aircraft dragged itself, heaving and panting, up from the runway into the air.

What happened over the next several hours remains one of aviation's greatest mysteries of all time. There is no official record, of course—only Corrigan's own word about the astounding events that followed.

Beaming with confidence and pride—his picture already in all the papers—Corrigan settled back inside the quaking cockpit for the long, bumpy ride back west. There was no radio, and the main compass on the control panel was out of order. His only functioning directional device was a smaller compass attached to the floor, which he could hardly make out from his angle.

A few hours out, Corrigan later revealed, strange things started happening. First, the plane drifted into a chilling blanket of fog that never seemed to lift. Then, just when he thought he should be over New Mexico or Arizona, instead of warm sunshine and soft clouds, he ran into snow and ice.

By then he had been airborne some twenty-six hours, a matter that greatly troubled the wayward pilot. Then, dipping low to get a bearing, he spotted something that made his blood run cold—a vast expanse of ocean, with nothing but windblown crests as far as the eye could see.

Without panicking, Corrigan simply figured he had missed the Los Angeles airport and somehow shot out over the Pacific Ocean. But this ocean looked strange—"not blue and calm the way the Pacific is supposed to," he thought.

Curious, he decided to keep on going "until I either sighted land or ran out of gas."

Some figs and chocolate were the only food on board—"the most delicious meal I ever tasted."

Corrigan pushed onward, without benefit of either radio or compass. Finally, just when his engine began sputtering, he spotted land—green hills and green fields and green forests. "It was the most beautiful sight I had ever seen," he related. "Yet, I still didn't have the foggiest notion where I was."

Beyond the hills lay a large coastal city, which Corrigan later admitted to recognizing immediately. It was Dublin, Ireland! Somehow, this bumbling, amateur aviator piloting a ramshackle monoplane with nothing left but fumes in his fuel tank had flown all the way across the Atlantic Ocean from New York to Dublin, Ireland—all without benefit of either radio or compass!

Corrigan had no difficulty landing the airplane at Baldonnel Airport. After taxiing to a stop near a hangar, he crawled outside the cockpit, stiff and cold from the twenty-seven-hour flight, and announced who he was and the unbelievable mission he had just accomplished.

"I am Douglas Corrigan," he reportedly told startled onlookers. "Just got in from New York. Where am I? I intended to fly to California."

The next day, with thousands of well-wishers looking on, Corrigan was officially welcomed as a hero by the Irish prime minister and by the American ambassador to England, Joseph P. Kennedy. When he returned to the United States, he was given another tumultuous hero's welcome, in spite of his "mistake" in navigational skills.

Amid ticker tape and parades and speeches, some found

Corrigan's incredible story too hard to believe. Just how had a third-rate pilot with no map-reading skills or transatlantic experience managed to fly so far off course—and survive?

While "Wrong-Way" Corrigan's antics were hailed by millions of Americans, the Commerce Department was not amused. He was held in "open detention," had his pilot's license temporarily revoked and watched while government workers dismantled his plane as punishment.

Was it all a hoax? Had Corrigan deliberately set out from New York to cross the Atlantic, just as he had always dreamed, following in the footsteps of his hero Charles Lindbergh?

Lie detector tests affirmed he was telling the truth. So did investigations by police and aviation authorities. "Anybody can make an honest mistake," he told a newspaper reporter.

Half a century later, while reassembling his plane for display at a small airport in California, he reportedly told another reporter that the flight had been a mistake all along. When asked if he was being honest, "Wrong-Way" Corrigan grinned and said, "I was never really known to be honest, you know."

Douglas "Wrong Way" Corrigan went to his grave in 1995 with the secret of his amazing flight still shrouded in mystery.

George Armstrong Custer

Golden-haired son of the Morning Star

The American West produced a number of larger-than-life heroes, but none cut a more striking figure than George Armstrong Custer, the dashing young Civil War commander and headstrong Indian fighter who died with 225 of his men on a wind-swept hillside overlooking the Little Bighorn River on June 25, 1876.

No other soldier in American history has been more lionized and scrutinized than this tall, handsome cavalry officer with the flowing curls, oversized cravat and trademark buckskin jacket. So many books, articles, plays and movies have appeared about him and his legendary Seventh Cavalry's famous "last stand" that it has become almost impossible to separate fact from fiction.

Part of Custer's mystique centered on his personality. Picturesque and magnetic, the young officer seemed to possess that rare quality which, in spite of his eccentric style and harsh discipline, attracted men who were willing to follow him anywhere—even to their death. As with George Washington and other great military leaders, men signed up with Custer just to be near him, to touch him, to see him in action, from the smoky heights of Cemetery Ridge to his final glory at Little Bighorn.

Custer's career didn't begin on such a brilliant note, however. Born in New Rumley, Ohio, on December 5, 1839, he graduated from West Point in 1861 at the bottom of his class. Ironically, the man who would become the youngest general in the Union Army narrowly avoided dismissal from school for misconduct by volunteering for service when the Civil War broke out.

Because of his bravery and uncanny skill in leading troops into battle, Custer rose quickly through the ranks. He first came to the attention of General George B. McClellan when he grew tired of listening to superior officers debate how deep the Chickahominy River was and rode his horse into the water to settle the question. Impressed by the junior officer's straightforward approach, McClellan had him appointed an aide.

During cavalry actions that followed—Gettysburg, Yellow Tavern, Winchester, Cedar Creek and Waynesboro—Custer so distinguished himself under fire that he was promoted directly from the rank of lieutenant to brigadier general.

But Custer was as reckless as he was daring. "That's a good trait for a cavalry officer," General William T. Sherman once remarked about his subordinate, whose abiding goal in life seemed the pursuit of fame and glory as he charged into battle, saber held high, golden hair flowing around his broad shoulders.

Custer's crowning glory during the Civil War probably came on May 11, 1864, when his regiment broke through Rebel lines and routed General Jeb Stuart, killing the flamboyant Confederate general in the process. Later, during the final phase of the war, he led Federal troops pursuing Robert E. Lee's battered and broken Army of Northern Virginia.

On April 9, 1865, it was George Armstrong Custer who received a Southern courier bearing the news that General Lee wished to surrender to General Grant and end the war in Virginia. Custer was later one of the officers present at the McLean house when the Confederate capitulation was worked out.

After the war, Custer—the consummate cavalryman—went on to become perhaps the most famous Indian fighter in American history. In 1874, the colorful general, clad in his familiar embroidered shirt and buckskin jacket, led an expedition of one thousand soldiers, miners and journalists into the Black Hills, the tribal land of the Sioux, where rumor had it there were rich gold deposits. The Indians protested the "invasion," but authorities in Washington refused to yield.

The reconnaissance had tragic consequences for the Indians. When Custer's prospectors confirmed there was gold in the Black Hills streams and that timber was abundant in the well-watered land, a spectacular land rush ensued.

Resentment flared as whites came into contact with the aborigines. When an attempt by Washington to purchase the land failed and Indians went on the warpath, the Seventh Cavalry was sent in to quell the disturbance.

Few people know that Custer had hired four Sioux, thirty Arikaras and six Crows as scouts. One of those Crow scouts was White Man Runs Him, who, legend has it, informed Custer that the Sioux's village was too large for the Seventh Cavalry to attack and asked him to wait for reinforcements. Custer refused, however, for fear the Sioux would escape and thereby deprive him of the victory he so desperately wanted and anticipated.

When Custer later noticed one of the Crow scouts taking off his uniform and putting on traditional Indian dress, he asked for an explanation. Speaking through an interpreter, the scout replied: "We are all going to die today, so I intend to meet the Great Spirit dressed as an Indian, not as a white man."

According to the story, the Indian's reply so angered Custer that he fired all the Indian scouts on the spot—thus, none of them died with the general.

When Custer left on his fateful march, he was only thirty-seven years old. Although his scouts had reported large bodies of hostiles in the region, Custer tended to downplay the threat. Even had he known the exact number of the enemy, it is doubtful he would have altered his tactics, so convinced was he that a hammer blow against any group of Indians would scatter them.

On June 25, 1876, he came upon an encampment of Sioux and Cheyenne, their tepees spread out along the valley of the Little Bighorn. Characteristically, he ordered the charge. Without waiting for the remaining elements of the proposed three-pronged attack and apparently fearful that he might have to share some of the glory, he led his men into a fray in which they were outnumbered eight to one.

Major Marcus Reno, a fine officer with a good Civil War record but with no Indian fighting experience, was sent across the valley floor in a direct attack while Custer took up position along the low-lying hills. For reasons still unclear, Reno broke off his attack and retreated instead of charging the camp.

Meanwhile, Custer moved his small but elite unit down from the hills, presumably to join in the attack he thought was taking place on the village. He didn't get very far.

On a grassy knoll overlooking the meandering river, Custer ordered his men and officers to take up a defensive position. Their stand was gallant and, some say, brilliant—but doomed from the start as some two thousand painted warriors on horseback swept up the gently sloping terrain, eventually overrunning the golden-haired general and his Seventh Cavalry.

Ignatius Loyola Donnelly

The "King of Kooky Cranks"

Toward the end of the nineteenth century, much of the scientific world was abuzz with startling new theories, many of them quite fanciful, on the history and evolution of the world and the myriad forms of its biological inhabitants.

In 1864, for example, a French scholar and cleric named Charles Brasseur de Bourbourg had come across a mysterious Mayan treatise that he believed offered conclusive evidence that an ancient continent called Mu had once existed in the Gulf of Mexico and western Caribbean.

Fueled by Brasseur's findings, another Frenchman, archaeologist Augustus le Plongeon, set out to prove that colonists from Mu sailed to Egypt and Yucatán, where they recorded their history and erected great temples. Both Brasseur and Plongeon believed that at the height of its power some ten thousand years ago the continent exploded and sank to the bottom of the sea.

Reports of yet another ancient landmass had been inspired by Charles Darwin's theory of evolution, which sought to explain, among other things, how various species of animals and plant forms had traveled from one corner of the world to another by using now submerged land bridges. Philip Sclater, a zoologist, called one of those lost lands Lemuria—which he believed was home to an advanced race of people who eventually colonized parts of Asia, the Pacific islands and western North America.

Sclater's notion was supported by many prominent scientists of the time, including Alfred Russell Wallace whose own theory of evolution matched that of Darwin. Even Sir Charles Lyell, the century's leading geologist, suggested that a volcano-dotted fracture at the bottom of the sea called the Mid-Atlantic Ridge might rise to the surface at some time in the future and become a powerful commercial and political base.

Such was the state of scientific speculation when a short, stocky, red-haired American businessman-turned-politician named Ignatius Loyola Donnelly sauntered upon the scene with compelling new evidence for the existence of yet another fabled continent—Atlantis. The story of Atlantis actually began with the Greek philosopher Plato, who wrote that an ancient realm once existed "far beyond the Pillars of Hercules" (the Straits of Gibraltar). About twelve thousand years ago, so Plato reported, disaster struck the mighty kingdom, causing it to sink beneath the waves in a single day.

Donnelly's fascination with the fabled lost continent would result in a carefully crafted book called *Atlantis: The Antediluvian World*. In spite of its scholarly shortcomings, *Atlantis* became an international bestseller, eliciting the praise of William Gladstone, the English prime minister. By 1890, more than twenty-three editions of the book had been printed and sold in the United States alone, and twenty-six in England.

To Donnelly, Atlantis was the world that had preceded the Biblical flood. Situated somewhere far out in the Atlantic, the Atlantean kingdom had been the Garden of Eden, the Elysian Fields, the home of powerful kings and queens who were later to become the gods of the Egyptians, the Greeks, the Phoenicians, the Hindus, the Scandinavians and the American Indians.

The people of Atlantis, Donnelly wrote, were a handsome, prosperous, technologically advanced people who worshipped the sun. Their oldest colony was probably Egypt, whose civilization reproduced that of the mother kingdom. The Atlantean alphabet inspired that of the Phoenicians, believed by many to be the parent of all European alphabets.

But all was not well on Atlantis, Donnelly pointed out. Society deteriorated as corrupt politicians led the population down the road to depravity and decadence. One day the entire island—along with most of the people—was destroyed by a series of earthquakes and tidal waves.

When Atlantis perished "in that terrible convulsion of nature," a few citizens escaped in ships and on rafts, bearing the dreadful news to the nations of both East and West—hence, the stories of the Great Flood that are told all over the world. As Donnelly saw it, these Atlantean refugees laid the seeds for the creation of many new civilizations—in Egypt, in India, in Central America and elsewhere.

Although his controversial book catapulted him to fame and fortune, life had not always been so kind to the dreamy Philadelphian. Until he withdrew from politics to write about Atlantis, Donnelly's life had been one long roller-coaster ride of ups and downs.

Born in 1831 to impoverished Irish immigrants, Donnelly became a lawyer and entered politics in his early twenties. In 1856 he moved to Minnesota, where he and a friend tried unsuccessfully to develop a metropolis grandly dubbed Nininger City. The city failed, so once again he turned to politics, first as lieutenant governor, then, three years later, as a United States congressman.

In the late 1870s, Donnelly ran afoul with post-Civil War political turmoil and dropped out of politics altogether. On his forty-ninth birthday—broke, dispirited, his political ambitions in tatters—Donnelly sat down and wrote, "All my hopes are gone, and the future settles down upon me dark and gloomy, indeed."

Little did he realize at the time that his future was about to take off in a radically different direction.

As a congressman in Washington, Donnelly had often spent hours each day in the Library of Congress pouring over the latest books and scientific journals dealing with geology, history, folklore, world literature, religion and linguistics. It was there that the idea for a book about Atlantis began to take shape.

He was drawn specifically to the many ancient similarities between the Old World and the New World—botanical, biological and cultural. Why, he wondered, did so many American and European animals and plants look alike? Why the coincidence of pyramids, pillars, burial mounds and ships appearing on both sides of the Atlantic?

Donnelly's answer was that everything had originated on the great continent of Atlantis. "I cannot believe," he wrote, "that the great inventions were duplicated spontaneously...in different countries. If this were so, all savages would have invented the boomerang; all savages would possess pottery, bows and arrows, slings, tents and canoes; in short, all races would have risen to civilization, for certainly the comforts of life are as agreeable to one people as another."

Everywhere he turned, Donnelly seemed to find corroboration for his developing Atlantis theories—even in the scientific literature of the day. For example, Otto Kuntze, the famed German botanist, had written that the principal domesticated tropical plants of Asia and the Americas—such as the banana—had first been cultivated in Atlantis, then transplanted to their modern habitats along with surviving colonists.

As popular as his vision of the lost continent was on both sides of the Atlantic, Donnelly knew his research was incomplete. What he needed was tangible evidence.

"A single engraved tablet dredged up from Plato's island would be worth more to science, would more strike the imagination of mankind, than all the gold of Peru, all the monuments of Egypt, and all the terra-cotta fragments gathered from the great libraries of Chaldea."

Encouraged by the favorable reception of his book and lectures, Donnelly reentered politics and twice ran for the vice-presidency of the United States on the ticket of the Populist Party he helped found. Although his political success was at a dead-end—and his critics called him "the prince of cranks"—the former land speculator, legislator, lawyer, political reformer and literary eccentric had laid the groundwork for his successors in a new field of study: Atlantology.

In 1888, *Atlantis* was followed by another equally successful book, *The Great Cryptogram*, in which he sought to prove that the plays attributed to William Shakespeare were actually written by Francis Bacon. His last major work, the popular *Caesar's Column*, published in 1891, forecast dirigibles and television and predicted world catastrophe unless economic and political reforms came about in the United States.

He died in 1901 at the age of seventy.

Isadora Duncan

"This woman is an outrage!"

*W*hen Isadora Duncan burst upon the world stage in the late 1800s—poised, barefooted, shimmering in her trademark headband and diaphanous Greek costume—the world wasn't ready for her.

"This woman is an outrage, scandalous, a threat to all decent societies," thundered one prominent New York dance critic. "She should be locked up at the earliest opportunity or, at worst, exiled to her beloved Europe along with other low-minded infidels."

But the beautiful young woman with the lithe body, graceful movements and bohemian spirit refused to be stilled, as she clicked, swirled and fluttered her way into the hearts of sophisticated audiences from London and Paris to Budapest and St. Petersburg. In Munich they showered her with flowers. In Paris art lovers went wild with enthusiasm for this barelegged American beauty with flowing robes and veil.

From Athens to Rome, Isadora Duncan danced as though in a trance, and her audiences sat thrilled, chilled and breathless. What if she did dance in scant veils that showed the honest beauty of her form? "There can be no evil in honest beauty," she once told a reporter.

Ironically, when she died at the age of forty-nine in a freakish automobile accident, Isadora Duncan, unarguably the most flamboyant dancer to ever grace the stage, was virtually unknown in her homeland. That was because most Americans did not share her shockingly revolutionary notions about nudity and "free expression" on stage. New Yorkers, especially, condemned her "modern" dance form and blasted her unorthodox lifestyle.

For years, critics in New York, San Francisco and other cultural centers in America had denounced Duncan as an artistic clown, a loose-living revolutionary and Communist menace whose loose attire and even looser style threatened conventional mores. The fact that she threw herself into affairs—even bearing illegitimate children—with the same reckless abandon she showed onstage did little to endear her to late Victorian audiences at a time when dance was defined by ballet's tutus and toe shoes.

One of her staunchest defenders was Theodore Roosevelt. "Isadora Duncan," proclaimed the president of the United States, "seems to me as innocent as a child dancing through the garden in the morning sunshine and picking the beautiful flowers of her fantasy."

In 1900, however, weary of all the criticism, Isadora packed her bags and caught a cattle boat to Europe. There, her spontaneous interpretive movements, barefooted performances and scandalous attire shocked and amused continental audiences, but made her an overnight sensation. Fame and fortune followed. So did more affairs that kept the art world on both continents buzzing.

Born in San Francisco in 1878, Isadora began dancing almost as soon as she could walk. By the age of six she had formed a "dancing school" for neighborhood children. At ten she dropped out of school to become a professional dancer.

A shy, dreamy child, Isadora loved poetry, beauty and rhythm. She loved to read, especially stories and myths about ancient Greece. Her great love for the classical world, in fact, helped inspire her appreciation for dance. But not just any dance. Toe-dancing, ragtime and jazz dancing were out. Too primitive, she felt, unfit for pure artists.

"I prefer natural, unaffected, spontaneous self-expression, unrestrained by rule and custom," she said.

Isadora's childhood was an unhappy one, due mainly to her parents' stormy marriage. Her father, Joseph Duncan, was a suave, cultured banker and connoisseur of the arts who clashed constantly with her mother, a "virtuous, high-principled Victorian lady" who demonized Joseph as a brute and a scoundrel. When Isadora was twelve years old, she made a solemn vow never to marry.

Isadora dreamed of getting away. There were distant horizons awaiting her, exciting challenges and people to meet. After her parents divorced, she talked her mother into moving to Chicago.

When she tried to get a job dancing, theater managers praised her talent but lamented her unacceptable style.

Then it was off to New York for another shot at her dream. It was there that Isadora began to develop her unique, highly personal style of expressive dance—a style neither in the tradition of formal ballet nor in keeping with standard musical comedy practices. One night Isadora danced to the music of Ethelbert Nevin. An art critic approved of her performance and—suddenly—New York was hailing a "new star, a child with the wisdom of the ages and the simple innocence of the sheep that grazed on the Athenian hills."

But Isadora's fame—and fortune—was short-lived as shocked audiences dwindled. As quickly as her rise to fame had been, so was the plunge from the top. Soon she and her mother were broke and had to sell everything they had just to eat—including several of Isadora's favorite dancing costumes.

From New York, they sailed to London, where a few engagements brought in a few dollars but hardly enough to fill empty stomachs. A chance meeting with Mrs. Patrick Campbell, the idol of the London stage, was a triumphant turning point in Isadora's life. The older entertainer was swept away by the young American's talent and highly imaginative style. She introduced her to London society—including British royalty. Overnight, Isadora's star rose dramatically. After years of heartbreaking struggle, she had arrived.

From London to Budapest, Duncan quickly established herself as a revolutionary dance artist. Newspapers and critics praised her unorthodox style, hailing the free-spirited Yank as a new "champion of freedom of expression in art and life-styles."

Behind the scenes, however, another revolution in lifestyles was going on. When it was revealed that Isadora had two illegitimate children by two different men, condemnations began pouring in. Romantically and professionally, her reputation began to sag. By 1913 Isadora's career was all but over.

That same year tragedy struck when her daughter and son drowned when the car in which they were sitting accidentally rolled into a river. Wracked by grief, Isadora withdrew from society, occasionally emerging to perform only dances of sorrow. During a rare performance in Italy, she met an Italian sculptor and soon had another child.

In 1921 she accepted an invitation to visit the newly established Soviet Union, where she fell in love with a half-mad poet named Sergei Esenin. This time Isadora bowed to convention and married Esenin, even though he was rumored to be seventeen years her junior. Another rumor circulating at the time suggested that the marriage had been arranged so that it would be easier for the poet to accompany her on a visit to the United States.

The tour was a total flop—due mainly to Isadora's insistence on baring her breasts on stage. Criticism steadily mounted. When she couldn't take it any longer, she and her young husband returned to Europe. After several violent quarrels brought on by financial setbacks and Isadora's heavy drinking, the couple separated.

A year later, in 1925, Sergei Esenin committed suicide.

Once again, Isadora Duncan slipped into a dark cloud of depression. Penniless and alone, she turned more and more to the bottle. But when word reached her in Italy that an American publishing house was interested in doing a new book on her, the fading dancer's spirits soared. For the first time in a long time she had reason to smile.

Bright and early on the morning of September 14, Isadora went to a nearby automobile dealership and asked to test drive an expensive sports car. The salesman on duty was only too happy to oblige the still-attractive celebrity.

While a crowd gathered to see them off, Isadora slid into the car and threw a long red shawl around her neck. In dramatic fashion, she waved to the crowd and said, "Goodbye, my friends, I go to glory."

A few minutes later the long shawl, trailing outside the open car, got caught up in a rear wheel spoke. With a few quick revolutions, the shawl tightened and broke the dancer's neck. She died instantly.

Isadora Duncan's tragic death shocked the world. "Those who loved her and knew her dream of beauty mourned this passing of a human creature who had been an honest builder of dreams," noted dance critic Samuel Dickson. "Isadora Duncan did more for the art of dance than any other man or woman in history. ..."

An expatriate for most of her adult life, Isadora is usually considered more a product of Europe. But Ann Daly, author of *Done Into Dance: Isadora Duncan in America*, sees her exile as heightening her relationship with America.

"Isadora Duncan set the agenda for modern dance in America, defining the terms and literally setting the practice in motion," Daly said, adding: "Duncan wanted more than to produce art; she tried to legitimize dance as a 'high' art. She also attempted to create and express a purely American dance form, which rejected the visual spectacle of ballet for a more 'natural' expression."

Marcus Garvey

The man who would be king

"When Europe was inhabited by a race of cannibals, a race of savages, naked men, heathens and pagans, Africa was peopled by a race of cultured black men who were masters in art, science and literature."

So proclaimed Marcus Garvey, a Jamaican-born black nationalist who moved to New York City in 1916 at the age of twenty-nine to become the leader of an international back-to-Africa movement that continues even today to inspire men and women of African descent. Garvey's message, coming as it did during America's racially troubled postwar period, appealed enormously to working-class blacks who felt disenfranchised by the liberal white establishment and black middle-class leaders.

By 1919, tens of thousands of African-Americans, mostly from the urban North, had warmly embraced Garvey's seductive call for black unity, while some three million strong had joined his Universal Negro Improvement Association, an organization that glorified all things black.

In time, most Negro leaders would come to denounce Garvey as a "buffoon," an insincere, selfish imposter. Some, like W.E.B. Du Bois and other leaders of the National Association for the Advancement of Colored People, went so far as to brand him a "lunatic," complaining that Garvey's re-colonization schemes cramped the cause of Pan-African movements.

But thousands more hailed him as the true leader of the Negro race, often comparing him to Jesus Christ. His movement was especially appealing to ordinary black people, especially Southern "field Negroes" and impoverished ghetto dwellers in Northern cities.

"I see a great ray of light and the bursting of a mighty political cloud which will bring you complete freedom," Garvey promised his people in a letter written in prison in 1923 shortly after his arrest and conviction on mail-fraud charges.

"Garveyism," as his movement came to be called, had less appeal among "house Negroes" of the black educated classes. This stratum was generally more attracted to the work of the National Association for the Advancement of Colored People and to the work of activists such as Dr. W.E.B. Du Bois.

In a blistering counterattack against the NAACP and other elements of the elitist black middle-class intelligentsia, Garvey accused his enemies of conspiring to "mix the races." The NAACP, he trumpeted, "wants us all to become white by amalgamation, but they are not honest enough to come out with the truth."

To be a Negro, he continued, "is no disgrace, but an honor, and we of the UNIA do not want to become white. We are proud and honorable. We love our race and respect and adore our mothers."

The basis for Garvey's wide popularity was his appeal to race pride at a time when Negroes generally had so little of which to be proud. Disillusioned by job discrimination, urban slums, disenfranchisement, lynchings and segregation, blacks saw themselves as victims of a white-dominated world that offered little or no opportunity for advancement.

The strain and stress of living in such a hostile environment created a state of mind upon which Garvey, a powerful, spellbinding orator, quickly capitalized. Calling himself the "black Messiah," Garvey exalted everything black. He insisted that black stood for strength and beauty, not inferiority, and he asserted that Africans had a noble past.

"We Negroes should be proud of our ancestry," he proclaimed. "God and Jesus Christ were black."

In his newspaper, *Negro World*, Garvey blasted white Americans and white Europeans, calling them liars, thieves and hypocrites. He called on the world's blacks—especially those of dark hues—to join forces in creating a political empowerment that would enable African people to reclaim their homelands from European powers.

"Let us return to Motherland Africa," he wrote, "and establish a nation strong enough to lend protection to the members of our race scattered all over the world."

Garvey took pleasure in bedecking himself in ornate, regal uniforms, complete with plumed hat, brass buttons and saber, and commissioning paramilitary orders with exotic names such as "The Dukes of the Niger," the "Universal Black Cross Nurses," "Knights of the Nile" and the "Black Eagle Flying Corps." Wherever he went, thousands followed, many mesmerized by his hypnotic oratory and the colorful parades, flags and uniforms.

Even veterans in the fight for racial equality were influenced by Garvey's magic. Du Bois himself once intoned: "The spell of Africa is upon me. The ancient witchery of her medicine is burning in my drowsy, dreamy blood."

The effect of the Garvey doctrines on the "unlettered and inexperienced Negro urban element, recently removed from the farm, was magnetic," wrote John Hope Franklin and Alfred A. Moss, Jr., authors of *From Slavery to Freedom.* "And what did he say? The only hope for Negro Americans was to flee America and return to Africa and build up a country of their own."

For example, at a UNIA convention at Madison Square Garden in 1920, the charismatic separatist told twenty-five thousand delegates: "We are the descendents of a suffering people. We are the descendents of a people determined to suffer no longer. We shall now organize the four hundred million Negroes of the world into a vast organization to plant the banner of freedom on the great continent of Africa. ... If Europe is for Europeans, then Africa shall be for the black peoples of the world."

On another occasion he boasted: "I was determined that the black man would not continue to be kicked about by all the other races and nations of the world. My young and ambitious mind led me into flights of great imagination. I saw before me...a new world of black men, not peons, serfs, dogs and slaves, but a nation of sturdy men making their impress upon civilization and causing a new light to dawn upon the human race."

While preaching that blacks should be proud of their race, Garvey told them to separate themselves cleanly from corrupt white society.

"I am the equal of any white man," he frequently declared, urging that blacks avoid using hair straighteners, skin lighteners or any other products that made them look white or otherwise distorted their natural looks and heritage.

In 1919, Garvey opened a consulting firm to assist black entrepreneurs. At the same time, he founded a chain of grocery stores, restaurants and other black-controlled businesses. His crowning achievement was the Black Star Line, a steamship company formed by black investment capital. If blacks desired to return to Africa, Garvey would provide them with the means to get there.

But to launch the steamship line, Garvey needed capital—lots of it. After consulting with friends, he seized upon the idea of forming an investment company in which blacks could purchase shares of stock for as low as five dollars each. Company brochures offered "easy dividends" to black investors—as well as an opportunity to "climb the ladder of success."

In November 1919, the BSL launched the first of its three ships, and stock sales soared. For a while, things looked promising for the confident leader of "Negro Zionism," the strutting, self-styled savior of the black race who already billed himself as the "first provisional president of Africa." The money continued to pour in, while the West African coastal state of Liberia anxiously awaited the arrival of the first transplanted colonists.

But Garvey's fevered dream of a black maritime empire in Africa was not to be. High operating costs, poor corporate management and large capital outlays soon doomed the enterprise. Adding to his woes were the constant poundings he took from the black "establishment" press that accused him of adventurism, opportunism and "diversion from the real paths of progress."

The assaults on Garvey's character and "questionable" motivation continued. None other than Du Bois called him "the most dangerous enemy of the Negro race," although he was uncertain whether the loud little man in the plumed military hat was a "lunatic or a traitor."

But hard times were just beginning for Garvey, the once-heralded "Black Moses." In May 1923, he and three associates went on trial for mail fraud in connection with the sale of BSL stock. In spite of an impassioned defense—masterfully staged by Garvey himself—he was found guilty and sentenced to five years in prison.

A federal appeals court upheld the conviction, and on February 8, 1925, Garvey began serving his five-year term at the Atlanta Federal Penitentiary. Two years later, under pressure by black and white groups that had protested the severity of the sentence all along, President Calvin Coolidge commuted Garvey's sentence but promptly deported him to England. Although deportation under such circumstances was required by U.S. immigration law, some historians have argued that Garvey's crimes hardly warranted his harsh judicial fate. "The popularity of black nationalism unnerved whites who were accustomed to a passive black population," summarized one scholar, while another blamed "atrocious bookkeeping" practices for the appearance of impropriety that led to Garvey's eventual downfall.

Without its charismatic leader, however, the UNIA quickly collapsed, along with the colorful parades, uniforms and the hopes and dreams of a generation of poor urban blacks. As for Garvey himself, he slipped into obscurity and died in England during a bombing raid in 1940 at the age of fifty-two.

Despite the exotic and romantic nature of Garvey's crusade and his ultimate failure, he convinced thousands of black Americans, especially the poor and discouraged, that they could join together and accomplish something and that they should feel pride in their heritage and their future.

"The widespread interest in Garvey's program was more a protest against the anti-Negro reaction of the postwar period than an approbation of the fantastic schemes of the Negro leader," commented historians Franklin and Moss. "Its significance lies in the fact that it was the first mass movement among Negro Americans and that it indicated the extent to which Negroes entertained doubts concerning the hope for first-class citizenship in the only fatherland they knew."

On the other hand, Marcus Garvey had done something no other black leader before him had been able to: serve notice that blacks had their own aspirations, which they could and would translate into action.

Shortly after his death, Harlem's largest newspaper, the *Amsterdam News*, summed up Garvey's continuing appeal to African-Americans: "In a world where black is despised, he taught them that black is beautiful. He taught them to admire and praise black things and black people."

Jay Gould

The most hated man in America

To some he was the most hated man in America. But to others he was a genius, a wizard, a god. "Nobody," boasted a lifelong businessman companion, "can make money the way Jay Gould does."

Jay Gould.

Even today, the very name conjures up smoky images of shady deals and fast bucks, multimillion-dollar maneuvers and diabolical takeovers. Perhaps no other figure in American history has generated so much antipathy or been the target of so much criticism, not even the most despised of labor leaders, radical agitators, social reformers, hardened criminals, political bosses or axe murderers.

"His touch is death," fumed one old enemy, while another called him "the worst man on earth since the beginning of the Christian era. He is treacherous, false, cowardly and a despicable worm incapable of a generous nature."

Even Joseph Pulitzer, the fair-minded publisher of the *New York World*, branded Gould "one of the most sinister figures that have ever flitted bat-like across the vision of the American people." Not to be outdone, another New York editor declared that "he should be called the Skunk of Wall Street, not one of its ubiquitous Wolves and Wizards."

Perhaps the crowning insult came in the pages of a respected English financial: "To attempt to sketch the character of Mr. Jay Gould in its true colors would be futile, since no language is equal to the task. ..."

"I do not believe," hissed Robert G. Ingersoll, the silver-tongued "Great Agnostic," "that since man was in the habit of living on this planet, anyone has ever lived possessed of the impudence of Jay Gould."

In almost every respect, Jay Gould seemed to personify the stereotypical "robber baron," a term to describe the small cadre of unscrupulous bankers and industrialists who emerged from the smoke and ruins of the Civil War to amass vast personal fortunes. While some, like J. Pierpont Morgan, John D. Rockefeller, Andrew Carnegie, James Mellon, Philip Armour and Cornelius Vanderbilt were twisting arms and engineering wars and rebellions to pile up fortunes in banking, oil and industry, Jay Gould led the pack in creating an empire founded on the transportation business.

But Gould was different. In an age of excess, marked by lavish social functions and Falstaffian appetites for food and drink, this shy, soft-spoken man who did not smoke, drink or swear, preferred solitude or the company of his wife and children, whom he carefully screened from the press. He avoided clubs all his life and refused to become "one of the boys."

Recognizing the difficulties his antisocial ways posed for him, Gould once admitted frankly that he had "the disadvantage of not being sociable. Wall Street men are fond of company and sport. ... My tastes lie in a different direction. When business hours are over, I go home and spend the remainder of the day with my wife, my children, and my books. Every man has normal inclinations of his own. Mine are domestic. They are not calculated to make me particularly popular in Wall Street, and I cannot help that."

Frail of stature and wracked with consumption, Gould was a loner, a shadowy figure who darted from opportunity to opportunity, never failing to turn every situation to his own advantage, regardless of the consequences to the enterprise or his associates. To much of the public, Jay Gould was a man of mystery about whom swirled the wildest rumors.

Born on a farm near Roxbury, New York, in 1836, Gould experienced a rise to fame and fortune that reads like an Horatio Alger novel. The son of a poor dairy farmer, Gould was attracted to books and numbers at an early age. While still in his teens, his mastery of business principles landed him jobs as a bookkeeper in a blacksmith shop, clerk in a country store and county surveyor.

At the age of twenty he gained control of a tannery—an operation he eventually sold at a considerable profit. According to legend, one of his partners was driven to suicide following Gould's takeover of the tannery. This incident, true or not, would haunt Gould for the rest of his life, helping shape his reputation as a cold and cruel profiteer.

Examples of Gould's genius for making money were numerous and legendary. At the height of the Civil War, while working as a Wall Street broker, his uncanny talent at turning profits enraged and bedazzled other titans of industry who were busy exploiting the crisis to build their own empires. Although little is known about Gould's activities during these years, it is clear that he mastered the intricacies of financial and corporate manipulation.

In 1868, following a fight with transportation king Cornelius Vanderbilt in which he bribed numerous officials, Gould was elected director of the Erie Railroad. During the next decade he undertook a number of ventures that astonished even hardened observers on Wall Street.

In 1869, for example, he engineered a scheme to corner the nation's gold supply. While bribing treasury officials as well as the brother of the president of the United States, Gould launched a relentless bidding war that drove the price of gold skyward. The result was the "Black Friday" (September 24, 1869) scandal that forced thousands of gold speculators into bankruptcy while further enriching Gould and a handful of co-conspirators.

By 1879 Gould had become one of Wall Street's most feared operators. He had shown himself to be both a technical genius and a bold visionary capable of thinking and acting on a scale unimagined by most men. According to one observer, "He saw possibilities that eluded less subtle minds and moved with lightning speed to realize them. His movements seldom went in a straight line. Like a chess master grasping the game several moves ahead of his opponent, Gould masked his every step in secrecy and subtlety.

"He thrived upon the confusion bred by his unorthodox strokes, and he possessed the patience to see every game through to the end."

Part of Gould's phenomenal success lay in his ability to manipulate men, the media and the courts to achieve complete control of a company. Once in command he would deliberately "de-arrange" its finances to suit his own needs.

"His mismanagement of an enterprise was a deliberate, calculated course of action," noted one historian. "Having wrung maximum personal profit from the company, he would gracefully retire, leaving in his wake a gutted and bankrupt enterprise."

During the early 1880s, Gould acquired the properties that became the basis for his personal fortune. From railroads like the Western Union, the Kansas Pacific, the Union Pacific, and the Texas and Pacific, Gould moved naturally to ownership of the telegraph industry and urban rapid-transit companies. He also purchased magazines and newspapers like the *New York World*, the same paper he would later sell to archenemy Joseph Pulitzer.

It was easy for critics to denounce Jay Gould as a robber baron or industrial pirate. Like other "captains of industry," he defied the law, ignored social and business custom and cared nothing for the enterprises he exploited and frequently wrecked. Unhampered by ethical restraints, he ruined adversaries by resorting to deceit and stealth. In short, he seemed to take everything and give nothing in return.

But it could be argued that Gould did give something in return. His great talent lay in gaining control over weak, unprofitable properties—the Erie, the Union Pacific, the Wabash and the Southwest lines of the 1880s are good examples—and turning them around. Consumers, shippers, the industry and, ultimately, the expanding young nation benefited from better services and lower transportation rates.

In a sense, then, even a buccaneer like Jay Gould made a positive contribution.

But Jay Gould's scandal-laden world began to crumble with the death of his beloved wife, Helen, in 1889. That, coupled with his own declining health, made his final years painful ones. While business struggles continued, his main fight was with tuberculosis, the disease against which he had fought so hard all his life.

He died on December 2, 1892, leaving behind a fortune conservatively estimated at $72 million. Ironically, in a little over a generation, his survivors squandered nearly all that Gould had amassed in his meteoric career.

Hetty Green

The "Wicked Witch" of Wall Street

$\mathscr{F}$or years, the shabbily dressed woman with the unkempt hair and wild look in her eyes was a familiar sight at New York's Chemical and National Bank where she came each day to count her cash and dividends. Clad in her customary rags and munching a raw onion, she would lock herself inside the vault until she'd finished tabulating her assets, sometimes taking all afternoon, even if it meant forcing bank employees to stay past closing time.

No one dared complain, however, for this eccentric customer, clad in Quaker black and wearing a perpetual frown on her face, was none other than Hetty Green, the legendary "wicked witch of Wall Street," reputedly the richest, meanest woman in the country.

On more than one occasion, Mrs. Green had seen to it that those who crossed her wound up in the unemployment line—or worse.

Next to counting money, Hetty Green's favorite pastime seemed to be bringing people down—destroying them, in fact, whenever and wherever it suited her. No one seemed safe from her wrath. Tellers, clerks, secretaries, even high-ranking officials of the bank trembled at her approach and tried to stay out of the old woman's way whenever she marched into the vault demanding to see her money and books.

Meanness apparently ran deep in Mrs. Green's blood, as did miserliness. As a child, she had grown up listening to her wealthy parents—Edward and Abby Robinson—talk only about money. Dinner-time conversations centered exclusively on financial matters, and her father was reputedly so tight he once refused the offer of an expensive cigar out of fear he might like it and lose his taste for cheap brands.

The Robinson family had come by its money the old-fashioned

way—through inheritance. Both of her grandfathers had made vast fortunes in a variety of ways—farming, trading with Indians, slavery, land sales, rum, Russian iron, merchant marine and, most of all, whaling. Her mother, born Abby Howland, was a "blue-blood" original, tracing her ancestry to the Mayflower.

Regardless of their enormous wealth, however, the Robinsons continued to heat their home with grate fires. They ate leftovers and simple meals prepared in a Colonial-style kitchen. They re-used matches and rarely bought new clothes except when absolutely necessary.

Hetty learned the meaning of frugality and the basics of managing money at an extremely early age. While other girls her age were playing with dolls, Hetty's father saw to it that his "little blue-eyed angel" was mastering the art of negotiating and learning about stocks and bonds and many other topics essential for running a successful business. By age six she could read the daily financial papers to her father. Two years later she opened her own savings account with the nickels family members sometimes gave her as rewards.

According to legend, the first sign of Hetty's own miserly ways surfaced at her twenty-first birthday party when she refused to light the candles on her cake because she didn't want to waste them. She was finally talked into lighting them but quickly blew them out so she could take the candles back to the grocer for a refund!

Years later she would economize by writing checks on scraps of paper instead of using blank forms. She also went to bed before sundown to avoid having to burn candles. One popular story holds that she spent all night searching for a two-cent stamp she had misplaced.

At age twenty-one she inherited seven and a half million dollars. On June 14, 1865, her father died, and Hetty inherited his vast estate, rumored to be at least one hundred million dollars. She became a familiar sight on Wall Street, and her natural astuteness with money enabled her to multiply her inheritance many times.

She continued to live frugally, often eating in "Pie Alley," where the main meal of the day cost just fifteen cents. She moved from place to place, bought secondhand clothes, rarely staying in one place long enough to pay property taxes. With her money and good looks, however, she was a constant target for young men seeking courtship. She refused to date, convinced that her suitors were only after one thing—her money.

It wasn't until she was thirty-three that she consented to marriage. The lucky suitor was a prominent New England businessman named Edward Henry Green, thirteen years her senior. A multimillionaire himself, mostly from trading in Asia, Green saw his marriage to Hetty as a convenient "arrangement."

Hetty Green's rise to infamy certainly had its roots in her childhood but apparently soared to new heights after her marriage. From the beginning, Green had sensed a shrewd business sense in his new bride and wanted to teach her the ropes about business. But he failed to anticipate the ragged side of his wife's soul, how she would stop at nothing to get her way, which usually meant controlling all the finances.

Within a year she had seized control of her husband's business, then booted him out when he acted against her advice about buying some railroad stocks. From that day on, Hetty Green's reputation as a cruel, tight-fisted operator grew by leaps and bounds.

When their son, Ned, was born, Mrs. Green swore to make him the richest man in the world. To achieve that, she started putting aside every nickel and dime for the boy's future. She never willingly spent a cent, not even for bills. When a dress got soiled, she'd wash only the part that was dirty in order to make the garment last longer. And when young Ned fell and broke his leg, Hetty refused to take him to a doctor because she was afraid he would "overcharge" her for the treatment.

Even though she had millions in the bank and owned at least eight thousand plots of land in New York City alone, she never paid a bill unless forced to. All her married life, she never owned more than a couple of ragged old dresses, a couple of shawls and hats, and a pair of shoes or two with worn-out soles. Most of the items had been purchased at secondhand stores. She never washed her underwear so it would last longer.

A quarrel over financial disagreements led to the eccentric couple's divorce in 1878. Hetty moved in with her son, while Edward took up lodgings in an inexpensive bachelor's club in New York City. Edward died in 1902 at age 82. From that day on, Hetty took to carrying a loaded revolver under her billowing black dress. She said it was to keep away lawyers.

Hetty continued to make shrewd financial decisions. In anticipation of the stock market drought of 1907, she withdrew her money from the bank and sold several lots of land. When the drought hit, many people came to her for loans, including large stores, businesses and even New York City. After that she loaned money to New York City many times, always extracting a "fair" interest on each loan.

Despite meager meals and a Spartan lifestyle, Hetty rarely got sick. On her seventy-eighth birthday she confided to a friend that she expected to live to be a hundred. She attributed her good health and long life to baked onions, which she chewed constantly.

In 1910, nearing the twilight of her bizarre life, Hetty Green turned all of her personal affairs over to Ned and went to live with a friend, Countess Annie Leary. For the first time since the birth of her son, Mrs. Green lived in decent surroundings. Until the countess took her in, it had been decades since the so-called "richest woman in the world" had enjoyed a three-course meal or slept in a clean, comfortable bed with silk sheets.

Even in the countess' house, however, Mrs. Green continued her ornery ways. Not only did she gripe about her friend's extravagant lifestyle—saying she would soon spend herself into the poorhouse—but constantly clashed with every member of the domestic staff.

When she fell out with the cook, however, a dour, ruddy-cheeked Dutch woman unaccustomed to taking orders, Hetty Green had finally met her match. In a heated exchange of words, the cook held her ground against the feisty old millionairess. Soon after the confrontation, Mrs. Green suffered a stroke—no doubt brought on by her battle with the cook.

There followed, over the next several months, several other strokes, each nibbling away at Hetty Green's once formidable strength. Her last years were spent in a wheelchair. On July 3, 1916, at the age of eighty-one, she died, leaving behind an estate valued at more than one hundred million dollars in cash, stocks and bonds, and real estate.

Always an ardent Quaker, Hetty was buried with her family in Immanuel Church's cemetery in Bellows Falls, Massachusetts.

Despite long and costly efforts by the state to collect taxes on the fortune, the "wicked witch of Wall Street" had the last laugh. Since she didn't own a home, it was impossible for New York State to establish residency.

As a result, Hetty Green went to her grave with her immense fortune intact.

Charles J. Guiteau

"His soul is in glory"

The nervous little man with the haunted stare and unkempt beard had clearly become a nuisance. For weeks he had been hanging around the White House, frightening staff members and occasionally dropping unsolicited notes into the hands of busy politicians.

When he started pestering Secretary of State James G. Blaine about a high-level appointment—preferably the consulship to Paris—staffers agreed it was time for him to go.

In a final fit of rage, Blaine reportedly cornered the uninvited visitor and roared: "Never bother me again about the Paris consulship as long as you live!"

Such a dressing-down might have discouraged most job seekers. But not Charles J. Guiteau, a forty-year-old unemployed lawyer, part-time evangelist, failed newspaper publisher and would-be Republican Party hack. The next day, in fact, Guiteau fired off a letter to President James A. Garfield demanding that he fire Blaine at once.

"Otherwise," Guiteau wrote, "you and the Republican Party will come to grief. ... Mr. Blaine is a wicked man, an evil genius...and you will have no peace till you get rid of him."

When Garfield ignored Guiteau's haughty request, an idea began to form inside the seedy little man's head. He would kill the president, after which he would be proclaimed a hero and savior of the Stalwart wing of the Republican Party, then elected by a grateful nation to succeed the deposed "traitor."

On June 16, 1881, less than a month before the planned assassination, Guiteau attempted to justify his "divinely inspired" scheme in an "Address to the American People."

"I conceived of the idea of removing the President four weeks ago. Not a soul knew of my purpose. I conceived of it myself. I read the newspapers carefully, for and against the administration, and gradually the conviction settled on me that the President's removal was a political necessity, because he proved a traitor to the men who made him, and thereby imperiled the life of the Republic."

In another passage, he charged that "the President's madness" had "wrecked the once grand old Republican Party; and for this he dies. ... This is not murder. It is a political necessity. ... I shot the President as I would a rebel, if I saw him pulling down the American flag. I leave my justification to God and the American people."

Later, on June 20, he added this even more bizarre postscript: "The President's nomination was an act of God. The president's election was an act of God. The President's removal is an act of God."

Early on the morning of July 2, 1881, Guiteau, armed with a silver-handled revolver that he kept carefully concealed in his coat, made his way through the crowd at the Baltimore and Potomac Railroad Station where the president of the United States was expected to arrive any minute. He smiled as he studied the crowd and the huge overhead clock, knowing precisely what he must do to save the republic and bring glory to himself.

Inside his pocket was a letter he thought would explain it all: "I have just shot the President. I shot him several times, as I wished him to go as easily as possible. His death was a political necessity. I am a lawyer, theologian and a politician. I am a Stalwart of the Stalwarts. ..."

So casually did he approach his fateful mission that he found time to go to the men's room and even to have his shoes shined.

It was in this delusional frame of mind that Charles Guiteau, the "Stalwart of the Stalwarts," was driven to fire two shots into the president's back as he walked arm-in-arm with Secretary Blaine toward his waiting train. The president, failing to respond to treatment, lingered two-and-a-half months before dying on September 19, 1881.

Guiteau's tragic deed not only ended the life of a president and plunged the nation into mourning for its fallen leader but brought into sharp focus the viability of insanity as a defense. While some of America's political assassins were clearly insane, others were motivated by political beliefs or dark personal desires.

"Normally," noted historian James W. Clarke, "it is difficult to determine where political partisanship ends and insanity begins."

Guiteau was "certainly unusual," continued Clarke. "Part conman, part religious fanatic, he believed he was destined for some sort of greatness. But was he insane? And, if so, was his insanity a legal defense for his actions?"

These and other questions had to be answered by the jurors who sat in judgment of Guiteau. In the end, however, judge and jury would ignore the assassin's obviously distorted view of reality and sentence him to death.

Charles Julius Guiteau, born in Freeport, Illinois, on September 8, 1841, grew up in an intensely religious family in which beatings were commonplace. From the beginning, people noticed that "little Julius"—as he was called until he changed his name in his teens—was different. Unruly, plagued by a speech impediment for which he was whipped by his stern father, Guiteau came to abhor physical labor, while developing precocious skills at reading and writing.

In 1860, with sex and the Lord on his mind, young Guiteau cheerfully entered the utopian religious Oneida Community in New York. Not long after his arrival, Charles came to believe that he had been divinely ordained to lead the community because, as he put it, he alone possessed the ability.

Charles soon found himself at odds with other members of the community—especially females—who disapproved and even ridiculed his high-handed, slothful and occasionally amorous ways. Adding insult to injury, they laughingly referred to him as Charles "Gitout."

Infuriated, Charles fled the community in April 1865, bound for New York City. With a new suit of clothes, a few books and a hundred dollars in his pocket, the nervous, squirrel-like little visionary planned to publish his own religious newspaper, which he was convinced would spearhead a national spiritual awakening.

"Whoever edits such a paper as I intend to establish will doubtless occupy the position of Target General to the Press, Pulpit, and the Bench of the civilized world," he wrote to his father. "And if God intends me for that place, I fear not, for I know that He will be a wall of fire round me, and keep me from all harm."

The scheme failed, however, when banks refused to loan him start-up capital. When another attempt at publishing failed, Charles decided to try his hand at evangelism. He had attended revival meetings in Chicago where the offerings had flowed generously. Impressed by the collections, the budding "minister of the truth" became convinced that, with proper advertising and promotion, he too could rake in the profits.

Adorned with sandwich-board posters, Guiteau walked the streets, inviting all who would listen to attend his sermons on the physical existence of hell and the Second Coming. The self-promotion was repeated in city after city—Milwaukee, Chicago, New York and Boston—where Guiteau's handbills proclaimed him "the Eloquent Chicago Lawyer."

The evangelical scheme fizzled as well when audiences either laughed or became angry at Guiteau's pitifully incoherent sermons, most of them lasting no more than fifteen minutes. The humiliated "minister" darted from town to town, leaving a trail of indignant audiences, unpaid bills and arrest records.

Describing himself as a "lawyer, theologian and politician," Guiteau next threw himself into the Stalwart faction's fight for the 1880 Republican presidential nomination in New York. Ignored, frequently ridiculed and occasionally chased away from party headquarters, Guiteau moved to Washington on March 5, 1881, where he began to badger not only the president's staff but Blaine and even the president himself in the corridors of the White House.

In a barrage of annoying "personal" notes written to Garfield, Guiteau begged for a job: "I think," read one such noted date April 8, "Mr. Blaine intends giving me the Paris consulship. ... I have practiced law in New York and Chicago, and presume I am well qualified for it. I have been here since March 5, and expect to remain some little time, or until I get my commission."

Guiteau became more persistent in pressing his claims for an appointment to the missions of Vienna, Paris or possibly Liverpool. He even informed the president that he intended to marry a "wealthy and cultured" woman—a woman he didn't even know—presumably to enhance his qualifications for a foreign ministry.

When no response was forthcoming, Guiteau wrote the president: "I have been trying to be your friend; I don't know whether you appreciate it or not. ..."

It was about this time that his assassination scheme germinated. Having drifted from one half-baked visionary scheme to the next his entire adult life, Guiteau now saw the way clear to the fame and recognition he had so desperately sought.

"Previously," explained Clarke, "Guiteau had accepted failure with remarkable equanimity, sustained always by the exalted opinion he had of himself. As one scheme after another collapsed—his leadership aspirations at Oneida, his journalistic ventures, the law practice, and the evangelistic crusade—his bitterness and disappointment were short-lived as he moved on to other careers."

On June 8, Guiteau borrowed fifteen dollars and purchased a silver-mounted English revolver. He planned to have it, along with his papers, displayed after the assassination at the Library of the State Department or the Army Medical Museum.

After several days of target practice and stalking the president—bypassing at least two opportunities to shoot him—he went into action on Saturday, July 2, 1881.

At his trial, George Scoville—Guiteau's brother-in-law—argued that his client was insane. Several aunts, uncles, cousins—not to mention his own mother who died of "brain fever"—were said to have suffered from mental problems. His own sister, Scoville's wife, would be institutionalized in October 1882.

"I have no doubt that masturbation and self-abuse is at the bottom of his [Guiteau's] mental imbecility," testified Guiteau's brother, John.

Throughout the seventy-two-day trial, Guiteau himself acknowledged that he was insane only in the sense that he had done God's will—not his own. "The Lord interjected the idea for the President's removal into my brain and then let me work it out my own way," Guiteau told the jury. "That is the way the Lord does. He doesn't employ fools to do his work; I am sure of that; he gets the best brains he can find."

Almost to the last, Guiteau believed he would be acquitted, at which point he would begin a lecture tour in Europe and later return to the United States in time to enter the 1884 presidential contest. When it became clear that he would not escape execution, he lashed out at the world, warning about divine retribution.

Before the noose was placed around his neck, he reminded those attending his execution that a monument was to be erected after his death, a monument inscribed with the words: "Here lies the body of Charles Guiteau, Patriot and Christian. His soul is in glory."

Harry Houdini

"No power on earth can restrain me"

$\mathcal{I}$n his day, Harry Houdini was unarguably the most celebrated entertainer in show biz, a man whose daring feats of magic and illusion touched millions. Before he died on October 31, 1926, the wizened old pro made a solemn vow—to somehow cross the threshold between life and death and return for his final act.

To this day, more than seven decades after his passing, Houdini's hopeful followers are still waiting. It's only a matter of time, they say, before the master returns—either in the flesh or in the spirit.

In 1990, for example, magic lovers, led by famed illusionist Kreskin, gathered in Marshall, Michigan, to attempt to communicate with the dead magician through mental telepathy and a series of séances. The effort failed, but Kreskin and others remain convinced that contact with the spirit world is possible.

Ironically, Houdini went to his grave claiming that spiritualism was one great big sham. He despised Ouija boards, psychics, clairvoyants, mediums and those who pretended to have connections with the spirit world because of an incident a few years earlier.

After his beloved mother died, Houdini spent a fortune trying to establish contact with her spirit through the services of a reputable medium. When every attempt failed, however, he grew bitter toward psychics and launched a strenuous campaign to expose trick séances. In time, he would even turn against his friend Sir Arthur Conan Doyle because of the writer's uncompromising views on spiritualism.

Houdini's return would have nothing to do with ghostly rappings, foaming strands of ectoplasm or other traditional tricks commonly associated with spiritual manifestations. Instead, the old master promised, his final feat would be accomplished through the miracle of his own craft—illusion.

At his funeral in 1926, thousands of devoted followers gathered inside the huge ballroom of the Elks Lodge on West 43rd Street to view their departed hero one last time. After the gleaming bronze coffin was sealed shut and taken away, many of those present expected to see the lid snap open any second and the familiar form within spring forth triumphantly to a standing ovation.

On this day, however, the master would disappoint the hopeful crowd. This time there would be no flourish of trumpets or drum roll or cloud of smoke. Harry Houdini, born Ehrich Weiss, fifth child of a Hungarian rabbi, the man who had cheated death thousands of times in the past with daring feats and dazzling illusions, was dead.

In many ways Harry Houdini was as strange and baffling as the magic he created. One moment he could be moody and withdrawn, scornful of the outside world; the next he could be charming and polite, bristling with energy and an obsession to become the best showman in the business.

His craving for success, a force that propelled him from abject poverty to tremendous wealth, had begun humbly enough when he went to work as a child to help support his impoverished immigrant parents. At the age of twelve, he worked in a sweatshop as a garment cutter. He also sold newspapers, shined shoes, worked as a meat cutter and took on other odd jobs to help put food on the table.

Young Ehrich was born on March 24, 1874, in Budapest. Although Houdini later claimed to have been born in Appleton, Wisconsin, he actually came to the United States when he was four years old. His parents, Rabbi Mayer Samuel Weiss and Cecilia Steiner Weiss, spoke only Yiddish, Hungarian and German.

Between jobs, Ehrich loved to perform "magic tricks." His first appearance before an audience was at the age of fourteen. "Ehrich, The Prince of the Air," performed as a contortionist and trapeze artist. He and his brother, Theo, teamed up to perform several acts at beer halls, amusement parks, as well as Chicago's World Fair in 1893.

Ehrich's fascination for magic and illusion drove him relentlessly. He studied hard and always tried to keep up with the top "magic acts" of the day. Early on, he knew how important it was to keep his body in tiptop shape so he could perform strenuous escape feats. He was an excellent athlete and won numerous awards in swimming and track. While still quite young, he bought a secondhand copy of a book on magic entitled *The Memoirs of Robert Houdin*. Houdin, a handsome, eccentric Frenchman, was widely recognized as one of the greatest magicians of the day. After devouring the book in a single sitting, Ehrich vowed to be just like the great French showman.

Some time later he learned that, in French, adding the letter "i" to a word meant "like." He decided to change his name to Houdini, hoping that he would one day be "like Houdin," his newfound mentor.

Like Houdin, Houdini was intrigued by escapology—the art of escaping from tightly bound ropes or other forms of bondage. He studied the craft religiously, finally mastering the secrets of rope escapes. He also taught himself how to swallow handfuls of needles; shed straightjackets, manacles and chains; and free himself from steel safes and a variety of other locked and secured spaces.

Before his twentieth birthday, Houdini went on the road, performing at county fairs, amusement halls, churches and anywhere else he could find an audience. He swallowed swords and escaped from trunks and chains. He performed sleight-of-hand tricks—anything, in short, to earn a dime and keep his vaudeville act going.

In time, Houdini came to be one of the most famous and highly paid entertainers in the world. But money no longer mattered. The great Houdini now lived for his "art" as he performed before mobs of adoring audiences from London and Paris to New York and Chicago. Nothing, it seemed, could prevent the tousle-haired magician from escaping the impossible.

In his most popular performances, Houdini hung suspended from tall buildings, bound and locked inside straitjackets or sacks. While crowds of hushed spectators watched from below, the master would slip free and gracefully descend a supporting rope or cable.

In 1894, Houdini met the love of his life—Wilhelmina "Bess" Beatrice Rahner, a young Jewish girl from New York. They married two weeks later.

The next year the young couple began working for Welsh Brother's Circus for $20 a week. The work was extremely hard but helped the young magician fine-tune his skills. While Houdini gave free performances and magic shows to attract crowds, Bess worked as a singing clown. Later, they presented a "second sight act," followed by an "escape from a trunk trick."

To garner publicity, Houdini boasted that "no power on earth" could restrain him—not ropes, tape, locks, even chains. He even offered rewards, often parading up and down in front of police stations and newspaper offices to attract attention to his daring challenge.

Houdini's life changed dramatically when a booking agent discovered him. Thoroughly impressed, the agent hired him on the condition that he abandon standard magic and focus on escape acts. That suited Houdini just fine. He went to work right away perfecting old skills and creating new acts. Soon a new form of entertainment was born—"The Challenge Escape." Harry Houdini, billed as "the most famous magician of all time," headlined theaters from New York to London. Ever the showman, Houdini often set up the audience to believe he may have died during an act, only to make his dramatic escape at the last moment.

The strenuous demands of his work eventually took their toll on Houdini's small, well-muscled body. A blow to his rib cage during an act finally sent him to a Detroit hospital where doctors advised the grand illusionist to go home and rest a few days.

Instead, Houdini's magic show went on—day and night, week after week—until one day, complaining of stomach cramps, he admitted himself to Grace Hospital in Detroit for observation. His condition was quickly diagnosed as acute appendicitis, and doctors went to work immediately to remove the ruptured organ.

In spite of a gallant effort, the doctors failed. Toxins from the man's damaged appendix had already seeped into his bloodstream. A few hours later, Harry Houdini lapsed into a deep coma and died, just as the sun was rising over the dark waters of Lake St. Clair.

Some who were with Houdini at his death say he promised to come back. Just how that was to be accomplished wasn't made clear. "The master never revealed his secrets," one follower remarked.

Robert E. Howard

The tortured genius who walked alone

He was young and handsome, on his way to literary fame and fortune. But one summer afternoon in 1936, something snapped inside the tortured mind of Robert E. Howard, the creative but ill-starred genius behind Conan the Barbarian and countless other sword-rattling heroes of pulp fiction, and he walked outside his mother's house and blew his brains out.

Until that fateful day, Howard had been a rising young star in the highly competitive world of fantasy fiction, struggling alongside the likes of Howard Phillips Lovecraft, Robert Bloch and Henry Kuttner just to survive until they scored a hit. After years of rejection notices and only a handful of published short stories to his credit, things had finally started looking up for the young writer.

Magazine editors had started calling *him* for a change. Even a couple of book publishers had expressed interest in several outlines he had presented. In the close-knit world of fantasy fiction, dominated for years by Lord Dunsany and his imitators, the name Robert E. Howard was starting to mean something.

Then, inexplicably, the tranquillity of tiny Cross Plains, Texas, a wind-blown community in the middle of nowhere, was shattered by the sound of gunfire. Eight hours later, one of the town's most famous sons—and one of America's greatest writers of fantasy fiction—lay dead behind his house, the victim of an apparent suicide.

Robert E. Howard was only thirty.

His untimely death and the mystery surrounding it have haunted his legions of fans for more than half a century. Based on the writer's own typewritten suicide note and several other factors, no one disputes the notion that it was his own finger that pulled the trigger, that no one else was involved.

What troubles a lot of people, though, are the strange circumstances leading up to his death. Friends, fellow writers and fans over the years have long pondered those circumstances and, to this day, have failed to reach a consensus.

Was it fear of failure that finally drove this swaggering, hard-drinking man with wavy hair and bulging muscles to put the Colt .380 automatic pistol to his right temple that hot, humid day in June? Or was it just the opposite—fear of success? Some researchers have suggested the man was driven insane by the same tortured fantasies that gave life to his most celebrated fictional hero, Conan.

Those who knew him well, however, believe it was something else that eventually pushed him over the edge—his own mother, perhaps. All his life, young Howard had shared an unusually close relationship with his mother, deriving much of his encouragement, strength and happiness from her affection and literary recommendations. When she died after a lingering illness, Howard's world seemed to fall apart. Three times before, he had planned his own demise when her death appeared imminent, but each time the woman had rallied.

Finally, when a nurse told the grieving son his mother would never again speak his name, he acted. His final words, found on the typewriter in his study, were these enigmatic lines: "All fled—all is done, so lift me on the pyre; the feast is over and the lamps expire!"

Although Howard's death fell short of national headlines, thousands of people from around the world mourned his passing. Scores of colleagues and fans flocked into town to attend the funeral. Over the years, thousands more would come to remote Cross Plains to pay tribute to their fallen idol, to remember a man now regarded as one of the masters of the genre.

Just who was this reclusive and—at times—painfully shy young writer with the big ambition obviously overshadowed by his mother complex? Followers of Howard have been trying to figure that out ever since his death.

Howard suffered from isolation, minimal worldly experience, limited travel outside of Texas and a lack of access to big-city and university libraries. "I have lived in the Southwest all my life," he wrote, "yet most of my dreams are laid in cold, giant lands of icy wastes and gloomy skies, and of wild, wind-swept fens and wilderness over which sweep great sea-winds, and which are inhabited by shock-headed savages with light fierce eyes.

"With the exception of one dream, I am never, in these dreams of ancient times, a civilized man. Always am I the barbarian, the skinclad, tousle-haired, light-eyed wild man, armed with a rude ax or sword, fighting the elements and wild beasts, or grappling with armored hosts marching with the tread of civilized discipline, from fallow, fruitful lands and walled cities. This is reflected in my writings, too, for when I begin a tale of old times, I always find myself instinctively arrayed on the side of the barbarian against the powers of organized civilization."

An even greater handicap was his family situation. After the death of his father, a prominent pioneer physician, Howard became excessively attached to his mother, who encouraged his slavish devotion. As a boy he resolved not to outlive her.

All his short life, Howard dreamed of a world far beyond the dusty confines of his little hometown. Through the magic of his writing, Howard was able to bring that visionary, fire-filled world to literary life; this was his so-called Hyborian Age, a savage, barbarous time when magic was potent, when chesty heroes clutching swords and big-bosomed damsels lived according to their own personal codes.

Howard proposed that this age had glittered between the sinking of Atlantis, around 12,000 B.C., and the dawn of known history. A catastrophe wiped out Atlantis and Lemuria, whose survivors reverted to savagery. In time, these people built new civilizations, and by 10,000 B.C., the powerful empires of Acheron and Stygia, rife with sinister sorceries, had arisen in the western part of the main continent.

Northern barbarians, the Hyborians, overran Acheron. On its ruins, the conquerors raised Howard's "shining kingdoms." Another natural catastrophe later ended the Hyborian Age, whose history survives only in fragmentary form in myths and legends.

One character dominated that age—a man whose body was "an image of primal strength cut out of bronze," who liked his women full-bodied and complacent but spent most of his time "afire with the urge to kill, to drive his knife deep into the flesh and bone, and twist the blade in blood entrails."

That character, of course, was a man called Conan.

Conan the Barbarian, who stalked the earth twelve thousand years or so ago, was only one of Howard's many longhaired, sword-clanging protagonists. He was the most enduring, however, eventually finding immortality in the person of Arnold Schwarzenegger and the silver screen.

Critics agree that Howard was the grandfather of sword-and-sorcery fiction. During the early 1930s, he almost single-handedly redefined the genre. His characters—Conan, Solomon Kane, King Kull, black Turlogh and others—lived and fought in colorful, mist-choked worlds ruled by superheroes and supervillains.

In all, Howard wrote 160 stories and novels, of which about twenty-one centered on his brutish, slow-thinking hero, Conan.

But literary fame and fortune remained one or two steps beyond the struggling young writer. In spite of his literary output, he never earned more than about two thousand dollars a year from his writing, which by the standards of the 1930s was quite a fair living—though townsfolk often wondered when he was going to give up writing silly stories and settle down to a proper job in a local shop or in the oil fields.

It wasn't until the 1940s—nearly a decade after his death—that Conan and his barbarian hordes actually earned literary respectability. The big break came in 1966 when a leading paperback publisher issued the first of what was to become a hugely successful series of Conan adventure novels—not all of them written by Howard.

In many ways, Howard's short, dream-filled life was every bit as mystifying and frightening as anything he wrote. Born frail and sickly, he was forced to learn boxing at an early age in order to defend himself against other kids. He also took an interest in bodybuilding, which probably helped shape his interest in Conan. Another factor was his fascination with the rugged Southwest and the legendary virility and strength of the pioneers and robust savages that once populated the region.

Described as an imposingly tall, dark, brawny man with piercing blue eyes, Howard invented characters who were as much like himself as they were pulled from his extraordinary imagination. Howard's mentor and friend, fellow pulp-fiction writer Howard

Phillips Lovecraft, described him as "a lover of the simpler, older world of barbarian and pioneer days, when courage and strength took the place of subtlety and stratagem, and when a hardy, fearless race battled and bled...the real secret of [Howard's stories] is that he himself is in every one of them."

The one great love in Howard's life—other than his mother—was an attractive, feisty West Texas schoolteacher named Novalyne Price who, some say, was drawn to Howard because of her own not-so-secret writing aspirations. The couple's relationship was passionate but brief, lasting only two years. Some Howard fans theorize it was his own mother who drove the "star-crossed" lovers apart.

Under the guidance of his mother, Howard had started writing stories when he was ten, pushing himself ruthlessly on the typewriter day and night. When his first story was purchased by *Weird Tales* in 1924, the eighteen-year-old got down on his knees and thanked God he'd finally broken into print.

By his early twenties, Howard was the first author of serialized fiction to ever earn a living as a full-time writer. His characters were simultaneously terrifying and seductive—an immediate sensation with the readers of *Weird Tales*.

Although it was his serialized stories, dubbed pulp fiction by critics for their apparent lack of depth or import, that gave Howard his vast following—making him the most popular fiction writer in America from the late 1920s to the mid-1930s—he was a gifted poet and writer of Westerns.

Only twelve years after the publication of his first story, despondent over his mother's death, wracked by nightmares and undoubtedly pursued by the fiendish demons of his own fevered fantasy, Robert E. Howard lay dying in a pool of blood behind his beloved mother's house.

While most biographers and critics have viewed Howard as a crazed, borderline psychopath, a book by former girlfriend Novalyne Price-Ellis, *One Who Walked Alone*, portrayed him as a deeply sensitive and loving man.

"Stonewall" Jackson

The demon-haunted savior of the Confederacy

Of all the great heroes of the American Civil War, none stood taller than Confederate Lieutenant General Thomas "Stonewall" Jackson, the brooding, Bible-quoting philosophy instructor from Virginia whose odd personal habits and daring flank attacks made him a legend in his own time.

As Robert E. Lee's most trusted commander, no other general helped win more decisive victories for the South, and no other commander's death dealt a more serious blow to the Confederacy. In battle after battle, from Bull Run to Chancellorsville, this tall, bearded scholar with the gaunt, weathered face and steely-blue eyes would shock and dazzle the world with his brilliant, lightning-like cavalry strikes and punishing infantry assaults.

Behind the gallant image, however, lurked a man obsessed with weird ailments, peculiar dietary compulsions and a dark fear that evil spirits had taken control of his body.

At Virginia Military Institute where he taught, for example, Jackson became known as "Tom Fool" because of his personal eccentricities, which included constantly sucking lemons to ease discomfort of what he thought was an ulcer. Students and colleagues knew him as a dull, pedagogic professor who rarely smiled, but when he found something amusing, he would throw back his head, open his mouth and emit a frightening roar.

Throughout his life he struggled to overcome the belief that he was "out of balance," that the only way to correct the condition was to remain in a bolt-upright position with his organs held "naturally" on top of each other. For this reason, he rarely used chairs, preferring to keep his posture erect whether standing, sitting, lying in bed or riding horseback.

In battle, he often charged with one gloved hand held high over his head, allowing the blood to flow down into his body to establish equilibrium.

Wherever Jackson went—into the countryside for rest and recreation, or onto the battlefield—he always took along his prayer book and prayer table. A converted Christian since 1849, Jackson believed the war boiled down to a struggle between good and evil. In his own mind, he was a modern crusader conquering the forces of evil.

Concerned about a mysterious stomach ailment, he kept up a strict regimen of raspberries, milk, plain bread or cornbread and an endless supply of lemons that he sucked even in the face of enemy fire. He also undertook a rigorous physical-conditioning program, replete with running, rope climbing and booming shouts to expand his lungs.

His complaints, issued almost nonstop throughout his young manhood, included rheumatism, dyspepsia, chilblains, poor eyesight (which he treated by dipping his head, eyes open, into cold water for as long as he could hold his breath), cold feet, nervousness, neuralgia, impaired hearing, tonsillitis (which eventually required an operation), biliousness and a "slight distortion of the spine."

The conclusion reached by many is that Jackson was a confirmed hypochondriac. But at least one modern doctor suspects that he may have suffered from a fairly common and most uncomfortable condition known as diaphragmatic hernia, a breach in the diaphragm.

His odd ailments—real or imaginary—kept him apart from his high-ranking peers, who frequently questioned his faculties. More than one general doubted his sanity. A.P. Hill, Lee's best division commander, contemptuously called Jackson "that crazy old Presbyterian," once referring to him as a "slumbering volcano" who might erupt in some irrational act without notice.

Born in Clarksburg on January 21, 1824, Jackson was orphaned at age seven and raised by an uncle. He was a quiet boy but worked hard to overcome shyness and to compensate for a lack of natural brilliance.

"Whatever Jackson needed, he drew from deep within himself," noted Joseph T. Glatthaar, author of *Partners in Command: The Relationship Between Leaders in the Civil War*. "During the Mexican

War, for example, Jackson brazenly exposed himself to enemy fire on sundry occasions. He simply willed away fear."

His hard work earned him an appointment to West Point, where a classmate named Ulysses S. Grant once recalled that Jackson was a "fanatic" whose delusions "took strange forms—hypochondria, fancies that an evil spirit had taken possession of him."

After graduating from West Point in 1846, he served with distinction in the Mexican War, rising to brevet major. After the war he resigned his commission to become professor of "natural and experimental philosophy" and artillery tactics at VMI in Lexington. There, cadets frequently played pranks on Professor Jackson and ridiculed him behind his back.

Ironically, when war came, many of those same students would rally around their quaint old professor because of his extraordinary achievements in battle and levelheadedness under fire.

Jackson remained at VMI until Virginia's secession in April 1861 when he was given command of the First Brigade of Virginia Volunteers—later known as the famous "Stonewall Brigade." He earned his nickname while leading troops into battle at Bull Run on July 21, 1861, when General Bernard Bee is said to have remarked to his troops, "There stands Jackson like a stone wall. …Rally around the Virginians!"

His nickname soon because a household word. For the rest of the war, whenever Rebel troops marched or galloped into battle, they often invoked the name "Stonewall" Jackson to give them strength and courage.

After winning fame at the First Battle of Bull Run in May, Jackson began his masterful Shenandoah Valley campaign, one of the most brilliant in military history. Racing up and down the valley with his fast-marching infantry, Jackson beat three separate Union armies, causing the North to divert troops from General George McClellan's offensive against Richmond.

In June 1862, Jackson's brigade linked up with Lee's Army of Northern Virginia in the bloody Seven Days battles which succeeded in driving Federal troops from the outskirts of the Confederate capital at Richmond. He later shared in the Confederate victory at the Second Battle of Bull Run.

At one point Lee praised Jackson as his finest commander. "Your recent successes have been the cause of the liveliest joy in this army as well as the country," Lee said. "The admiration excited by your skill and boldness has been constantly mingled with solicitude for your situation."

The relationship between Jackson and Lee, though never intimate, was warm and respectful. "Theirs was a casual relationship," writes Glatthaar. It was "one rooted in an effective professional relationship rather than anything truly personal. Occasionally they socialized, but there was no strong bond between them. Neither Virginian could cast aside the cloak of propriety."

Quiet, secretive and still struggling with shyness, Jackson was a self-contained man who rarely shared his personal life with anyone except his wife and a small circle of friends. "There was a playful side to Jackson," wrote Glatthaar. "But only a chosen handful witnessed it."

Part of the general's reluctance or inability to interact socially with others most certainly stemmed from his bizarre outlook as well as the demands of the war itself. "The war, his struggle with sin, and family affairs consumed most of his day and left little time to cultivate congenial relationships," added Glatthaar.

Jackson's most daring campaign was his last one. On May 2, 1863, he led his 28,000-man army against a much larger Federal force of 70,000 men at the Battle of Chancellorsville. Launching several surprise attacks on the enemy where they least expected it, he was able to rout an entire wing of the Union forces.

Late that afternoon, however, while on a reconnaissance ride, Jackson was wounded by several of his own guards, who mistook him for an enemy officer. Three balls struck Jackson, one in his right hand, another in his left wrist and a third above his left elbow.

Following the amputation of his left arm, complications set in, and the legendary Confederate general died of pneumonia at Guinea Station, Virginia, on May 10, 1863. Only a few hours before, Lee had sent a note to Jackson that read: "Could I have directed events, I should have chosen for the good of the country to be disabled in your stead."

Lee later confided to a friend that Jackson "has lost his left arm, but I have lost my right."

Ironically, Jackson's own habit of covering his abdomen with cold towels in an effort to relieve pains of "dyspepsia" may have caused his death. According to some sources, he fully recovered from the amputation but died when pleurisy and pneumonia set in after an attending servant draped the wet towels over his body without the knowledge of his doctor.

Jackson's odd ways may have been foreshadowed at the First Battle of Bull Run when he was wounded in the hand—perhaps while holding it up in his quest for "body balance." When a surgeon recommended that several fingers be amputated, Jackson jumped on his horse and fled.

Marie Laveau

Cajun queen of the undead

*I*n her heyday, Marie Laveau was the undisputed monarch of American voodoo, a larger-than-life enchantress who controlled her subjects by blowing "magic dust" in their faces and by exploiting their fear of the unseen world.

When she died in 1881, thousands of black-robed disciples attended her funeral in New Orleans. But some say she never died, that the bones rotting inside her crumbling tomb at St. Louis Cemetery Number 1 on Basin Street are those of another, and that Marie Laveau, the exalted high priestess of the undead, still roams the shadowy bayous and cobbled streets of New Orleans in search of fresh blood.

To protect themselves from the powers of darkness, believers in voodoo seek the help of certain male priests called *hougons*, or their female counterparts, *mambos*. Long ago, authorities gave up trying to suppress the voodoo cult, a mystical, quasi-religious organization based on Laveau's interpretation of West Indian fetish worship and perverted elements of Catholicism.

Just as in Laveau's time, charms, herbs, talismans, powders, potions and other objects aimed at warding off evil spirits or otherwise controlling the supernatural world are still bought and sold freely on the open market today.

Voodoo—a word which means "spirit" in Fon and other languages of West Africa—arrived in Louisiana during French colonial times, along with thousands of black slaves from Haiti. But it was not until the arrival of Marie Laveau that the practice of this enigmatic religion blossomed.

Until then it was known that certain voodoo priests and priestesses possessed supernatural powers and knowledge of strange, mind-altering drugs and poisons. White masters were sometimes powerless, for example, when under the influence of voodoo spells, and there are some records of slave owners having actually been poisoned by drug-induced blacks.

According to most sources, Marie Laveau was born in 1794 on the Caribbean island of Santo Domingo, a former Spanish colony. Her early years remain shrouded in mystery, but it is known that she was a free woman of color, possibly the daughter of a wealthy plantation owner and a slave. She was raised as a Roman Catholic, the religion favored by most French and Spanish colonials at the time.

A tall, striking woman with fiercely burning eyes, Laveau began her trade as a fortuneteller and seller of charms, amulets and curses. Soon her rooms thronged with people of both races and every class who were willing to pay exorbitant sums of money for protection against evil spirits from the unseen world.

While she reigned supreme in New Orleans, no one was safe from her unrelenting powers—not even aristocratic white planters who often came to her in the dead of night for secret sessions involving voodoo and, some say, sex. Especially vulnerable, however, were the gangs of black slaves who sought her advice and protection. For these poor souls, most of them freshly transplanted from the jungles of Africa via the Caribbean, it was a world of darkness and unrelenting terror, a world filled with unimaginable nightmares.

Ghosts and goblins stalked the streets of the city and haunted the lonely woods and marshes. Angry voodoo gods were everywhere, but the most dreaded was Baron Samedi—known in some quarters as Three Spades. Three Spades was one of the *Guede* or voodoo death spirits that roamed the countryside, clad in black coat and stovetop hat and clutching a bloody shovel.

Voodoo had been present in New Orleans long before Laveau's arrival, but the law forbade it from being practiced openly. In 1782, for example, the Spanish governor declared it illegal to import slaves from Martinique because of its people's belief in voodoo. However, when New Orleans fell into American hands following the Louisiana Purchase in 1803, restrictions on slave importation were canceled. The result was a massive influx of immigrants from Santo Domingo, free and slave. Soon the squares and alleyways of New

Orleans and the surrounding swamplands echoed with the steady stamping of feet and the hypnotic sound of drums and shrill "voodoo chants."

The most popular gathering place in New Orleans for voodoo worshippers was Congo Square, where slaves performed traditional African dances, including the *Bamboula*, to the beat of primitive drums. They also performed other voodoo rituals, including the worship of *Damballa*, the snake god.

When Marie Laveau was twenty-five, she married a freeman of color, Jacques Paris. When Jacques died—some say he disappeared under mysterious circumstances—Laveau took up quarters with another man, Christophe Glapion. It isn't clear whether she married Glapion or not, but they had fifteen children. One of those children—also named Marie—was a dead look-alike for her mother.

Throughout her life, Laveau welcomed outsiders to her cult's annual festival of St. John's Eve in midsummer. But behind these public ceremonies, Marie Laveau presided over many secret meetings during which the real magic of voodoo was invoked and the wild ritual was carried to orgiastic extremes.

One of the most spectacular ceremonies occurred each June 24 when Marie Laveau would rise out of Lake Pontchartrain with a big communion candle burning on her head and one in each hand. With singing and chanting in the background, she would walk to shore where she then presided over the rites—which included more singing, chanting and frenzied dancing.

Whites were excluded from these meetings, which were usually held at her small, whitewashed house nestled beneath moss-draped oaks along the gloomy shores of Lake Pontchartrain. During services, the chief voodoo spirit—summoned by a *mambo* or *hougon*—would appear in the form of a serpent. By handling the snake, celebrants would receive messages from the spirit world.

After this preliminary phase of the ritual, the *loa*—or guardian angel spirits—would enter the priest and others, causing them to stagger, fall, spring up again, shake spasmodically, and, at times, lapse into hypnotic trances. Some participants say the *loa* mounted them or rode the persons possessed.

Other devotees danced, drank and chanted. There was more

chanting and dancing, more drinking and singing while the drums beat louder and the priests and priestesses moved through the swaying congregation members, slapping them, spinning them around, spraying them in the face with liquor from their own mouths. Some excited participants would roll among the crackling flames, unconcerned about their flesh peeling away, while others joined in sexual union, climbed trees, barked like dogs, mimicked, then drank the blood from sacrificed roosters and other animals whose bodies they tore apart and ate raw.

According to some stories, Marie Laveau was attended during such ceremonies by a huge rattlesnake that coiled around her arms and legs. The snake, which voodoo worshippers believed to possess magical, godlike powers, stayed near her side all her life. The day after she died, the rattlesnake supposedly crawled off into the woods and was never seen again.

Though the voodoo celebrations on the bayou were spectacular, they were more for show than as true religious rituals. The real voodoo worship seems to have been conducted in private homes.

Known primarily to history as a voodoo queen who used her powers to manipulate and acquire power, Marie Laveau also had a soft side. During an outbreak of yellow fever in New Orleans, for example, prominent citizens begged her to use her sorcery to heal the sick and ward off the plague. She also attended to the needs of prisoners awaiting execution on death row, bringing them comfort and gumbo, a traditional New Orleans seafood stew of African origins, and helped treat the American wounded at the Battle of New Orleans.

Some detractors condemned Laveau as not only a voodoo priestess but a baby killer as well. It was often alleged that she and her followers kidnapped children and cooked them—sacrifices to unholy gods. No credible evidence has ever been found to substantiate such charges.

An essential element of Laveau's magic was *gris-gris*, a French word meaning black and gray—loosely translated to mean "good" and "bad" magic. Good charms were called *juju*, while bad charms were called *mojo*. *Gris-gris*—a potion of herbs and other ingredients, including powdered brick, ochre, cayenne pepper, fingernail clippings, human hair and snakeskin—was the most powerful of all charms and also the most expensive.

Prior to Marie Laveau, others ruled the voodoo world in New Orleans. Three of the most famous were Dr. John, Dr. Yah Yah and an influential free woman of color and food peddler named Sanite Dede. She learned from all three and went on to become the most prominent figure in the true history of voodoo in America.

When she grew old, Marie Laveau attempted to inject elements of Roman Catholicism into her voodooism. Statues of saints, belief in the Virgin Mary and Holy Water were now mixed in with the snake, zombies and the *gris-gris*. Her efforts to reform voodoo did not set well with most of her followers, and eventually rival queens and voodoo doctors forced her out of power.

The memory of Marie Laveau lives on today in New Orleans, if only in legend. Each year thousands visit her grave to marvel and pray over the remains of the once-powerful voodoo queen. Some make the sign of the cross and leave offerings—beans, food, various voodoo items—but most silently agree the world is a safer place without her presence.

Huey Long

The demigod of Dixie

He was a good old boy from way down deep in Louisiana bayou country, and when a crazed assassin's bullet struck him down in his political prime on the night of September 8, 1935, there were those who confidently predicted he'd return one day, puffing on a long cigar and riding high on a cloud.

"Of course, he'll be back," snorted one Cajun crony when he learned that the Kingfish himself—Huey Long—had been shot point-blank in the stomach while strolling through the corridors of the state capitol in Baton Rouge. "And when he does, the poor will be eased of their burdens, and every man will be king."

Others swore that the Kingfish had somehow survived the shooting and was still alive. According to one account that circulated for years, the flamboyant and once-formidable senator had been whisked away to a secret chamber in the capitol where he was being kept prisoner.

Another claimed that he had been confined to a lunatic asylum somewhere in the city and that sometimes late at night when the wind was just right "you can hear him howling from somewhere inside the old State Capitol, where he seems to be making some kind of speech."

It was only natural that such legends would spring up about Huey Pierce Long, the rambunctious, back-slapping politicalmeister whose homegrown charm and carefully cultivated wit rendered him immensely popular among poor whites in the Deep South. To legions of loyal supporters, including Western farmers and Northern urban workers, Long was a hero, a grassroots demigod, a larger-than-life messiah who took pride in bucking big government and the liberal policies of his political nemesis, Franklin Delano Roosevelt.

Part of the Kingfish's enormous appeal stemmed from his vision of a new South ruled by and for the common man. In 1931, for example, when he entered the U.S. Senate race, he proposed a "Share Our Wealth" plan—a plan that advocated the seizure of all family fortunes of more than $5 million and a 100 percent tax on earnings larger than $1 million a year. These funds, he claimed, would help provide every family with an annual income of $2,000 to $3,000, plus a "homestead" consisting of a car, a house and a radio.

Long's plan, along with most of his other anti-aristocratic, anti-establishment views was understandably popular among the dirt farmers and factory workers of his home state. In 1936 the Kingfish claimed some 4.6 million members for the Share Our Wealth movement. It was with that kind of support that he began to entertain the idea of running for president, possibly as early as 1936.

Born in 1893 into a lower-middle-class farming family in rural Winn Parish in northern Louisiana, Long was a restless soul, always moving, always trying to "out-hustle" opponents. Bored with the backwoods, he ran away from home several times but always returned.

While still a youth, Long proved himself to be a glib and persuasive orator. For a time he made a living peddling books and other merchandise as a traveling salesman. He dropped out of high school but taught himself law and got a degree in that field after only one year of study. At age twenty-one he was admitted to the state bar, then won election to the Louisiana Railroad Commission four years later. He later became chairman of the state Public Service Commission.

For the next several years, Long waged a ceaseless campaign against the utilities, condemning them for overcharging the public and eventually forcing a reduction in rates. In 1928, campaigning before enthusiastic farmers with the slogan "Every man a king, but no man wears a crown," Long captured the Democratic nomination for governor.

Hard-driving and ruthless, Long swiftly clamped an iron hand around the state political machine. Under his autocratic rule, political opposition was all but stifled as enemies were intimidated, persuaded to come over or silenced. By taxing the utilities and oil companies to finance massive public works and social welfare programs, Long won the support of the people and made himself the virtual dictator of Louisiana.

"I'm the constitution around here," he proclaimed unabashedly.

And as for those who complained that he was incompetent to hold high public office because of his lack of education, the Kingfish proudly retorted: "It is true, I am an ignorant man. I have no college education. I have not even had a high school education. But the thing that takes me far in politics is that I do not have to color what comes into my mind and into my heart. I say it unvarnished. I say it without veneer."

Long's swift rise to power in Louisiana politics can be attributed to his remarkable skills as an orator, his capacity to organize and his tactics in ridiculing opponents. He blasted Wall Street, big business and the landed aristocracy of the Southern states as "Whistle-Breeches," a term that rarely failed to elicit howls of laughter from his folksy audiences. He became a determined enemy of the Roosevelt administration because he saw it as too beholden to these powerful forces.

Political enemies frequently described him as a demagogue—a label he roundly rejected.

"Some deceive the people in the interests of the lords and masters of creation, the Rockefellers and the Morgans," Long thundered. "Some of them deceive the people in their own interest. I would describe a demagogue as a politician who don't [sic] keep his promises."

He gave himself the nickname "Kingfish" because, he said, "I'm a small fish up here in Washington. But I'm the Kingfish to the folks down in Louisiana."

In 1935, the Kingfish mounted his drive for the White House. His prospects seemed good, thanks to his popularity and the success of his Share Our Wealth plan. In fact, one Democratic poll taken that year estimated that he could carry three to four million votes in 1936—enough, perhaps, to upset Roosevelt's bid for a second term. The results also indicated that, should the Depression continue, he would be a shoo-in in 1940.

But on the night of September 8, 1935, as he made his rounds through the dimly lit legislative corridors of the state capitol, a white-clad, bespectacled figure stepped out of the shadows from behind a pillar and approached him. Witnesses said the man, Dr. Carl Austin Weiss, pulled out a small-caliber pistol and fired once, striking Long in the stomach.

Weiss, who some say was upset because Long had helped arrange for his father-in-law, Judge Benjamin Pavy, to be fired from his job, was killed instantly in a volley of machine-gun shots fired by Long's bodyguards.

Mortally wounded, Long staggered down the stairs and into a car in the parking lot. Aides rushed him to a nearby hospital, but two days later Huey Long, the most successful demagogue in American history, was dead at forty-two.

Long's assassination sent shock waves across the nation. With the presidential election right around the corner, the fast-talking, wise-cracking senator from the Pelican State appeared to have been gaining ground on the incumbent president. Only weeks before, Long cornered a group of reporters and boasted, "Franklin Roosevelt will not be the next president of the United States. ...Huey Long will be your next president."

So confident was he that he wrote a book entitled *My First Days in the White House* in which he named his cabinet. Members included President Roosevelt as Secretary of the Navy and President Hoover as Secretary of Commerce. In the book, he also conducted long imaginary conversations with FDR and Hoover designed to humiliate them and show their subservience to the boy from the piney woods of Louisiana.

Most Americans, including members of the press, were accustomed to such lofty pronouncements from the cigar-chomping Kingfish, who enjoyed strutting around in pink suits, red ties and two-toned shoes and—in spite of his great intellect and oratorical skills—making people think he was a country bumpkin.

But many took him seriously. Longtime political ally Gerald L.K. Smith said, "As God is my judge, the only way they will keep Huey Long from the White House is to kill him."

Smith's strangely prophetic words had come to pass.

The official report indicated that Long had been assassinated by Dr. Weiss. But rumors were already circulating before the funeral that a conspiracy was behind the assassination, a conspiracy that reached far beyond Baton Rouge. Some investigators theorized that the deranged young doctor had been nothing more than an unfortunate fall guy for a sophisticated assassination plot that reached far beyond the state capital.

In the early 1990s, Professor James E. Starrs of George Washington University introduced new evidence that casts significant doubt over the historic account of the assassination. Starrs, who led a team of specialists in the exhumation of Dr. Weiss' body in 1992, suggested that the ill-fated doctor might not have killed Long after all.

"It is submitted that there is significant scientific evidence to establish grave and persuasive doubts that Carl Austin Weiss was the person who killed Senator Huey P. Long," Starrs was quoted as saying.

Since no autopsy was ever performed on either Long or Weiss (Long's bodyguards had emptied their guns into Dr. Weiss' body— 24 shots in all), some historians and Long supporters suspect that some sort of political conspiracy was, indeed, behind the assassination. More than one expert has come forth to intimate that Long was actually shot by bodyguards who were part of the plot.

For years, the case was clouded by speculation and contradictory accounts of witnesses. The disappearance of state police records and the actual weapon supposedly found on Dr. Weiss only deepened suspicions among conspiracy theorists that more was behind Long's death than mere revenge by a deranged doctor.

While the investigation continues, the memory of Huey P. Long lives on in the state of his birth, along with cult-like predictions of his "second coming." So revered is the Kingfish that a newspaperman once noted, "There would be a revolution in Louisiana, if anybody tried to move Huey Long's grave from the Capitol grounds at Baton Rouge."

Howard Phillips Lovecraft

At the mountains of madness

The early twentieth century saw the rise of some of the finest craftsmen who ever worked in the tradition of weird fantasy— Arthur Machen, Algernon Blackwood, Robert E. Howard, Seabury Quinn, Robert Bloch, Edmund Hamilton, Clark Ashton Smith, August Derleth and Lester del Rey, to name just a few.

But of all the great writers to leave their mark on the genre, none comes close to matching the renown and peculiar artistry of an eccentric young recluse named Howard Phillips Lovecraft, a pulp-magazine writer and part-time editor who died in relative obscurity in Providence, Rhode Island, more than half a century ago.

Today, Lovecraft's name, known around the world, has become synonymous with ghoulish beasts, creeping monsters and other unspeakable horrors lurking just beyond what he termed "the thin wall of darkness separating reality from the unplumbed gulfs of madness." He and his gruesome tales have appeared in at least one hundred anthologies and dozens of films and have been translated into twenty-five languages.

Before he died in 1937, this cult master of the macabre, who enjoyed sitting on tombstones, ranting about "inferior, slant-eyed foreigners" and taking long, solitary walks at night, wrote some sixty stories and novellas, most of them less than fifty-thousand words in length, which revolutionized weird fiction.

Drawing heavily upon the works of Edgar Allan Poe and his idol, Lord Dunsany of Ireland, Lovecraft worked hard at creating a unique style of literature that some modern critics have divided into three basic categories—Dunsanian fantasies, dream narratives and a singular literary phenomenon known as the Cthulhu Mythos. His biggest claim to fame, however, rests on the Cthulhu Mythos, a group of short stories, novellas and poems that blend elements of science fiction with weird fantasy.

Although Lovecraft started the Mythos, an ever-widening circle of writers has contributed to the series, including modern masters of horror such as J. Ramsey Campbell, Brian Lumley, Gary Myers, James Wade and Colin Wilson.

Behind the popular Mythos is this premise: Millions of years ago horrible demon gods from distant galaxies and dimensions came down to earth to dominate the steaming fens and fern forests of remote geological eras. In time, these ghoulish perversions of nature were driven from the earth by a race of kindly disposed Old Ones. Although imprisoned on far-flung worlds, the evil influence of the Ancient Outsiders lingers in certain repellent myths of frightful antiquity, and they are venerated by loathsome rites practiced by certain elder cults in remote backwaters of our planet.

According to essayist Lin Carter, himself a Mythos contributor, Lovecraft created the literary impression that "our age is…haunted by the fear that they [the demi-gods] may awake from the deathless sleep wherein they are imprisoned, break their fetters, and…return!"

It is this struggle between the demon "Outsiders" and vulnerable human beings that moves the Mythos stories along, often to horrifying conclusions.

Lovecraft's creations are buttressed by continuous references to invented sources—spurious quotations from rare texts of ancient lore, learned anthropological allusions and esoteric data gleaned from literary and archaeological studies. He further intrigues and baffles by mingling fact with fiction, scholarship with invention. He often cites passages from "forbidden" books like the abhorred *Necronomican*, written by the mad Arab Abdul Alhazred, as well as Ludwig Prinn's hellish *De Vermnis Mysteriis* and the infamous *Cultes des Goules* of the *Come d'Erlette*.

In spite of all his talk and tales about demon gods and cannibalism and rotting corpses in the earth, Lovecraft remained until his dying day a shy, frail and sensitive man, so squeamish he often fainted at the sight of blood. Once, after having caught a field mouse in a trap, he flung the whole thing away, trap and all, rather than touch the carcass—hardly what a true, blue-eyed, bloodthirsty Aryan berserker would have done!

To begin at the beginning, Howard Phillips Lovecraft was born on August 20, 1890, into a family descended from proud English stock. As a child, surrounded by doting female relatives, young Lovecraft withdrew into a bizarre dream world in which the peaceful green hills of New England were transformed into a weird landscape filled with the dead sounds of monstrous steps in the night, the rush of gigantic wings and obscene whispers that floated down from the stars and up from ancient, blood-soaked gravestones.

Shy and precocious, young Lovecraft was reciting poetry at age two, reading at age three and writing at age six or seven. His earliest enthusiasm was for the *Arabian Nights*, which he read by the age of five; it was at this time that he adopted the pseudonym "Abdul Alhazred," who later became the author of the mythical Necronomicon that figures in later stories.

Throughout his short life he loved cats and ice cream and Colonial architecture. He adored the eighteenth century, Republican Rome and the fantasy literature of Lord Dunsany, Blackwood and Machen. His hatred for foreigners—especially the "verminous hordes of distorted aliens" that flocked to New York—knew no bounds, as did his distaste for all things modern and mechanical.

And, even though he was married once, he avoided women and all things sexual, preferring the company of celibate young males like himself.

"Through it all," wrote Carter, "he lived most of his rather short life in a sort of self-imposed exile from his century, a recluse, something of an invalid, holding the world at arm's length and having little to do with people."

One critic called Lovecraft "a complex blend of neurasthenic invalid and Nordic superman; of arrogant poseur and lonely misfit; of cosmic fantaisiste and rigorous scientific materialist; of scholar, scoffer, and seeker; of life-hater, and lover who never found any object worthy of his love, or who never found himself worthy to offer love. ..."

After his marriage failed to Sonia Haft Greene—a Russian Jew seven years his senior—Lovecraft's only friends consisted of a handful of scholars, poets and writers with whom he stayed in constant contact through correspondence. It is through his letters, some of them more than fifty pages long, that much has been learned about this complex and enigmatic man who, even though he never published a single book and died a pauper, would become the most celebrated American writer of weird fiction since Poe.

Critics say it wasn't so much Lovecraft's style that eventually made him popular but his literary innovation and the unwavering commitment among a few friends to keep his work alive posthumously—most notably August Derleth, who founded a publishing company, Arkham House, for that purpose.

As Carter noted, "He [Lovecraft] has no ability at all for creating character, or for writing dialogue. His pose is stilted, artificial, affected. It is also very overwritten, verbose and swimming in adjectives. His plotting is frequently mechanical, and his major stylistic device, which becomes tiresome, is the simple trick of withholding the final revelation until the terminal sentence—and then printing it in italics, presumably for maximum shock value."

Although he was frequently asked by publishers to write full-length books, Lovecraft declined because he felt he lacked talent for such an extended commercial project. Instead, most of his short stories eventually wound up in the pages of *Weird Tales* and other pulp magazines that flourished during the 1920s and 1930s.

Lovecraft's earliest tales demonstrate not only a fondness for the uncanny and the macabre but also the slavish imitating of Poe. In 1917, for example, he composed a brief, very Poe-esque story called "The Tomb." Other stories followed, including "The Call of Cthulhu" in 1926 that launched him in an entirely new direction.

Some of his best stories arguably include "The Whisperer in the Darkness," "The Dream-Quest of Unknown Kadath," "Through the Gates of the Silver Key," "The Lurking Fear," "At the Mountains of Madness," "Dreams in the Witch House," "The Strange High House in the Mist," "The Outsider," "The White Ship," "The Moon-bog" and "The Shadow over Innsmouth." Most of these tales follow the Cthulhu line, summoning forth such dreaded creatures as Yog-sothoth, Hastur, Cthulhu itself and other lurkers in the earth and beyond the barriers of time.

In 1929 Lovecraft's stormy marriage to Sonia ended in divorce. Although he continued to profess affection for his former wife, his aunts—Lillian D. Clark and Annie E. Phillips Gamwell—saw to it that their troubled, sickly young nephew never saw her again.

The last two years of Lovecraft's life were filled with hardship. In 1936 his beloved Aunt Lillian died. A few weeks later one of his closest companions, writer Robert E. Howard, committed suicide. Depressed and lonely, Lovecraft checked himself into a hospital to treat pains in his stomach and limbs.

He grew rapidly weaker. By February 1937, emaciated, distended with gas and fluid, and often in great pain, Lovecraft was confined to bed. He continued to write, propped up on pillows, but the cancer that had invaded his intestines was so painful he had to be fed intravenously and frequently sedated with morphine.

He died early on the morning of March 15, pen and pad in hand. The death certificate gave the cause as "carcinoma of intestines, chronic nephritis." He was buried in the family plot in Swan Point Cemetery, among the same ancient trees and crumbling headstones he once wandered as a young man in search of inspiration for his own nightmarish visions.

Bernarr Macfadden

"Weakness is a crime"

$\mathscr{B}$ernarr Macfadden had every reason to believe he would live to the ripe old age of 120, just as he often predicted in the pages of the popular, health-oriented magazine he published during the early decades of this century.

Staying strong and healthy were the keys to longevity, he preached, and to that end the colorful publisher, international health guru and one-time hobo advocated limited sex and lots of exercise, rest and proper nutrition.

"Weakness is a crime," he wrote in the fitness magazine he launched in 1899, adding that those who allowed their bodies to turn to flab should be prosecuted.

Practicing what he preached, Macfadden exercised daily, fasted frequently and lived on a diet of nuts, carrots and beet juice. "Too much food is just as bad as the wrong kinds of food," the flamboyant millionaire declared. "The animals in the forest know how to eat. Watch them at it sometime. You can learn from them."

One of his favorite exercises was to stand on his head for long periods of time, saying it "toughened up" his spine, aided digestion and helped make his hair grow. Most mornings he was up before dawn, running and working out, insisting that those around him do the same—including his third wife whom he eventually divorced when "she did not follow my instructions as to her own body. I wanted her to be an example of my work and a credit to me."

Among the wifely duties evidently neglected by his wife—winner of Great Britain's "Perfect Woman" contest—were calisthenics at daybreak, followed by a ten-mile run.

Macfadden's curious claims and boundless energy helped make him a millionaire by the 1920s. His success with *Physical Culture* led to ownership of several other magazines, all of which made lots of money for the controversial publisher and self-styled health fanatic. While critics derided him as a "health nut," no one could dispute his genius as a magazine publisher. *True Detective Mysteries*, *True Story*— the first confession magazine—and *Fiction Lovers* were among the string of popular pulp periodicals that transformed his once-fledgling enterprise into a $30 million empire.

Ironically, Macfadden's life had not started out on such a cheery note. Born in 1868 to sickly parents—his father died of alcoholism in 1872, followed a few years later by the death of his mother from tuberculosis—Macfadden resolved early to keep body and mind fit. Orphaned and sent to work on an Illinois farm, he ran away at age twelve and became a hobo.

For years he wandered the open road, rode the rails and slept out under the stars, then finally settled down in the field of physical education. A pamphlet he wrote on health led to his first magazine, *Physical Culture*, which soon attracted a large readership.

The advertising success of *Physical Culture* led two decades later to the start of his second magazine, *True Story*, billed as a "journal about ordinary people and how they coped with their successes and failures." Macfadden himself was a frequent contributor to the magazine, often appearing in bogus photos he arranged himself.

Soon he was editing and publishing more than twenty periodicals, ranging from *Muscle Builder* to *True Detective Mysteries*. Much of his editorial formula included gratuitous amounts of sex and violence—tame, perhaps, by today's standards, but pretty hot stuff during the Depression-era years. One observer commented that his magazines were based exclusively on "sex and carrots."

He constantly battled against prudes and censors, especially Anthony Comstock and his successors. The American Medical Association also fought back, charging him with quackery and misrepresentation.

Married four times, Macfadden obviously considered himself enough of an expert to recommend that intercourse be used for procreation only. He also said babies should be born without doctors, suggesting that outsiders inhibit the bonding experience between mother and child.

Macfadden's wisdom, which touched and inspired millions of devoted fans around the world, extended to other areas as well, including how to beat cancer. The best way, he frequently wrote, was to eat grapes and drink lots of grape juice. Almost every issue of *Physical Culture* contained at least one article on the nutritional benefits of grapes.

Such notions got him a lot of media attention. *Time* magazine nicknamed him "Body Love" Macfadden, while other publications referred to him as the "Father of Physical Culture." Sometimes his creative efforts went too far, resulting in charges of obscenity. He was arrested several times after *Physical Culture* ran a series of photos that authorities deemed "inappropriate and lewd to the point of being pornographic."

Throughout his long life, he campaigned tirelessly against "pill-pushers," processed foods and prudery. Such charges drew heavy criticism from members of the medical community, who branded him a "kook" and a "charlatan." Never one to hold back, he tagged mainstream doctors who opposed him "losers" and "legal quacks and bandits."

A firm believer in self-sufficiency, he urged followers to secretly bury their money rather than deposit it in banks. Legend holds that some $4 million of his dollars remain buried in old ammunition chests scattered across the United States.

In his personal life, Macfadden's eccentricities and strong will were detrimental to several marriages. His most celebrated marriage came in 1913 when he went to England on a promotional tour to find "the most perfect specimen of English womanhood." He found her—Mary Williamson, a voluptuous brunette almost three decades younger than Macfadden.

Never one to miss an opportunity for publicity, Macfadden toured the country with his new wife, billing them as "the world's healthiest man and woman." They staged shows wherever they went, often attended by thousands of followers and curiosity seekers. As a grand finale of their act, Mary would climb to the top of a seven-foot-high ladder as Macfadden lay on his back directly underneath. Then, after the drum roll, she would jump directly on Macfadden's stomach and bound onto the stage.

The couple opened a health resort in Brighton, where Mary gave birth to the first of their six children. In 1915, with the outbreak of war in Europe, the Macfadden family returned to America, where they were greeted with a triumphant reception.

Macfadden succeeded in creating an image of his family as the perfect model of a physical culture family in which all members were healthy and happy because they followed his principles. But nothing could have been further from the truth. In reality, he was a tyrannical father who used his family to bolster his image and advance his own fame.

Mary complained once that she felt as if she had been kept perpetually pregnant. Throughout each pregnancy, she never was allowed to see a doctor because of her husband's uncompromising belief that people should be able to take care of themselves. As they grew older, his children often complained their father was mean and overly demanding.

The highlight of Macfadden's cruelty to his children was demonstrated one Christmas when he made four of his daughters put on skimpy costumes and dance in an outdoor Christmas program in Central Park. Such antics brought more criticism from the press, but Macfadden brushed it aside, claiming that "it was good for them." He also publicized the fact that none of them ever caught a cold.

Years later, however, Mrs. Macfadden revealed the truth—the children had become seriously ill from exposure to the extreme cold.

Not one to miss an opportunity, Macfadden campaigned for the presidency of the United States and twice ran for a U.S. senate seat. He also offered to be governor of Florida if the people wanted him to. They didn't. In fact, he was never taken seriously as a political candidate.

Until the end, Macfadden sincerely believed he'd live to be 120. He gave it a good try, flying planes and making parachute jumps as an octogenarian.

But at age eighty-seven, he contracted jaundice and had to be hospitalized for the first time in his life. He fought back gallantly, but even Bernarr Macfadden, the famed "Father of Physical

Culture," couldn't slow down the disease ravaging his body, no matter how hard he tried. One day the proud old millionaire slipped into a coma and, to the surprise of everyone, died. The year was 1955.

Ironically, his illness had been aggravated by one of Macfadden's own patented cures—a three-day fast! Had he obeyed his doctor's orders to eat, Macfadden might have recuperated and lived another thirty years.

Cotton Mather

The dark world of Salem's most famous witch hunter

The horror that came to Salem, Massachusetts, in the waning years of the seventeenth century was spawned in part by one man, an arrogant, hotheaded, and monumentally pompous clergyman turned witch hunter who passionately believed the Devil had invaded his beloved New England.

In 1686, Cotton Mather, son of the great Puritan leader Increase Mather and the most famous minister in New England at the close of the seventeenth century, had a vision in which God called upon him to combat Satan in the new colony on the edge of the frontier. After much fasting and prayer, Mather produced a polemic exposing "the whole Plot of the Devil against New England in every branch of it. ..."

Through books and fiery sermons, Mather declared that "prodigious Witch-Meetings" were being held all over the country at which "a fearful knot of proud, ignorant, envious and malicious creatures" volunteered for the Devil's services.

"An army of Devils," he concluded, "is horribly broke in upon that place which is the center, and after a sort, the first-born of our English settlements."

Confronted by these "horrible Enchantments and Possessions," Mather urged fellow colonists to join him in fighting the "plague of Witch-Craft" before it destroyed the Christian fabric of their new homeland.

"I believe," he said, "there never was a poor Plantation, more pursued by the wrath of the Devil, than our poor New England."

In Mather's mind, the Devil and his unseen agents were everywhere, riding the midnight wind, lurking in dark forests and fields, hiding in tightly shuttered homes and cabins throughout the land. Sometimes they were visible, but most often not due to their supernatural power to turn "spectral" at will or otherwise alter their physical form.

But at least the enemy's leader was identifiable. From reports he had heard, Mather pieced together a picture of the Devil: "a short and a Black man…no taller than an ordinary Walking-Staff," who wore "a High-Crowned Hat, with strait hair, and had one Cloven-Foot."

In May 1692, on the advice of Mather and other clergymen, Governor William Phips appointed a special court to investigate charges of witchcraft. So began the infamous witch trials of Massachusetts, a time in which hundreds of innocent suspects fell prey to the atmosphere of fear whipped up by Mather and his gangs of black-frocked, blue-nosed zealots.

In Salem alone twenty people would be executed—nineteen by hanging and one crushed to death beneath rocks. Scores of others would languish in prison until the frenzy finally passed. Meanwhile, no one was safe from the charges; to the witch hunters, any person could be in league with the Prince of Darkness. Husbands turned against wives, wives against husbands. Children charged their parents with practicing witchcraft.

The wife of the Reverend John Hale, secretary of the colony of Connecticut, was denounced as a witch, and one woman who was hung at Salem was a church member. Cotton Mather himself stood accused in October 1693 when a young woman swore his image threatened and molested her.

"I cried unto the Lord," Mather wrote in his diary, "for the deliverance of my Name, from the Malice of Hell."

Before a trial began, Mather personally interviewed numerous suspects in an attempt to determine in his own mind their guilt or innocence. In his *Memorable Providences*, he described certain symptoms found in some accused children: "Sometimes they would be deaf, sometimes dumb, and sometimes blind, and often all this at once.

"Some tongues would be drawn down their throats; others would be pulled out upon their chins to a prodigious length. They would have their mouths opened until such a wideness that their jaws went out of joint, and anon they would clap together again with a force like that of a strong spring-lock."

He continued: "They would make most piteous outcries that they were cut with knives, and struck with blows that they could not bear. Their necks would be broken so that their neck-bone would seem dissolved unto them that felt it. ... Yea, their heads would be twisted almost round, and if main force at any time obstructed a dangerous motion which they seemed to be upon, they would roar exceedingly. ..."

Some modern experts have concluded that the symptoms described by Mather were clear evidence of hysteria-convulsive movements, distorted postures and loss of hearing, speech and sight. But in Mather's day, such mannerisms could only be the work of the Devil and his unholy agents.

One woman, for example, told Mather that she frequently went to meetings where her "Prince"—the Devil—was present along with other persons whom she named. Then, according to Mather, the woman provided additional displays of possession. Her belly would swell "like a drum, and sometimes with croaking noises in it."

On another occasion, while Mather was praying with the woman, "there came a big, but low voice from her, saying, 'There's two or three of them [or us].' One of her more grotesque hallucinations was riding on a spectral horse.

Opinions about witchcraft in Massachusetts covered a full spectrum, ranging from wild-eyed citizens who accepted every unusual happening as an indication that "spectral forces" were at work, to those who sincerely doubted supernatural involvement. As for Mather, "spectral evidence" seemed hardly credible. From his pulpit each Sunday, he preached that "prayer, faith and a good life" were better at ridding the community of evil than were simple charms.

Historians have generally been harsh in their treatment of Mather for his role during the witch hysteria. True, the publication of his *Memorable Providences Relating to Witchcraft and Possessions* in 1685 helped fan the hysteria culminating in the witch trials of 1692. To his credit, however, Mather stood firmly against the death penalty for those convicted, urging prayer and fasting instead.

After the trials, Mather went on to publish more than 440 books and tracts on a wide range of topics, including *The Angel of Bethesda* in 1722, *Magnalia Christi Americana* in 1702 and *The Christian Philosopher* in 1721. Before he died in Boston in 1728, he amassed the second-largest library in North America with some forty thousand volumes.

James McGready

"Shouting out the devil" along the frontier

Following the great Indian wars of the late eighteenth century, waves of restless pioneers poured over the mountains into the new frontier. Thousands floated down the Ohio on fleets of flatboats, while others came in great convoys of ox-drawn wagons, clattering and rumbling through misty mountain passes on their way "up country" into Kentucky and Tennessee.

By 1800 more than a quarter-million people called Kentucky home At least half that number lived in Tennessee, while tens of thousands of other hearty immigrants swept into Ohio.

Still, the new frontier, with its dense forests and dark mountain ranges, remained a lonely and faithless place. Far removed from the familiar comforts and confines of the Tidewater, despairing men and women of the wilderness frequently turned their backs on civilization and adopted the ways of the Indian just to survive.

It was only natural that religion would come to play an important role in the lives of the people who inhabited this bleak and perilous world.

Beginning with the "Great Awakening" of the mid-eighteenth century, circuit-riding ministers belching "fire and brimstone" roamed the backwoods in search of lost souls. They came on horseback and on foot, solitary travelers mostly, bent on saving the wicked and the damned as they bravely trod the wilderness peddling Bibles and spreading the Gospel of the Old Testament. This march of faith across the frontier would continue for a century, peaking with the hysteria spawned by the "Great Revivals" of the first half of the nineteenth century.

The theme of these evangelical extravaganzas, which shook the country from New England to Kentucky, was fear—fear of judgment, fear of God's wrath, fear of hell. Powerful preachers reminiscent of Increase Mather, Jonathan Edwards, George Whitfield and James Davenport lashed out at packed congregations, whipping the flock into such emotional frenzies that many ordinary men and women, caught up in the spirit, sang and wept and danced and spoke "in tongues." Some jerked so violently they snapped their necks and died.

Of all the Bible-toting agents of the Lord to enter this wild domain, none was more successful than James McGready, a tall, angular Presbyterian who could "make Satan as real as a whooping Shawnee and hell more horrible than the stake."

Little is known about McGready the man, but frontier legend is full of the rowdy antics of this long-haired, bow-legged, fire-breathing evangelist whose personal struggle to bring salvation to the backwoods was often tainted with whispers of scandal and wrong-doings among the flock.

Born and raised in the hills of western Pennsylvania, McGready received his religious training from a farmer-preacher who appears to have been long on damnation and short on salvation.

Sometime around 1790, McGready set off for the mountains of North Carolina. Armed only with a tattered Good Book and a passion for "God's shining glory," the bristling young clergyman compensated for his lack of formal education with an instinct for exhortation. With wildly gesticulating arms, darting eyes and rolling thunder in his voice, he could move audiences to tears or send them thrashing and howling to the ground in a state of unrelieved ecstasy.

Thousands attended his open-air services just to be near him, to hear him, to gaze upon his holy presence with raptured awe. His words of redemption brought spiritually starved men and women who exhorted him to cleanse their souls and make them "pure as the Lamb." When McGready warned sinners to prepare for the "Awakening," untold thousands rushed to be baptized, while others sank to their knees, prayed and sang Jehovah's praises.

Not long after his arrival in Carolina, however, McGready ran afoul of local authorities. It isn't exactly clear what happened or why, but the young evangelist soon lit out for Kentucky. Legend has it he hurried away one dark and moonless night after receiving a threatening letter written in blood.

It was in the Kentucky backwoods that McGready's bellicose style took root and flourished. According to Presbyterian annals, the new preacher with the "dark, burning eyes...so arrayed hell and its horrors before the wicked" of Red River, Gasper River and Muddy River—three of Kentucky's more sin-filled areas—"that they would tremble and quake, imagining a lake of fire and brimstone yawning to overwhelm them, and the wrath of God thrusting them down the horrible abyss."

Even the "boldest and most daring of sinners" exposed to McGready's powerful sermons frequently cowered in fear, "covering their faces and weeping." McGready presented so formidable a presence at Gasper River in July 1799, for example, that many took "to falling to the ground, groaning, praying and crying for mercy."

An enormous crowd had turned out for the camp meeting, some arriving from as far as one hundred miles away. Convinced that God was moving among the congregation, McGready gave the following description of the event: "The power of God seemed to shake the whole assembly. Toward the close of the sermon, the cries of the distressed arose almost as loud as his voice. After the congregation was dismissed the solemnity increased, till the greater part of the multitude seemed engaged in the most solemn manner.

"No person seemed to wish to go home—hunger and sleep seemed to affect nobody. Eternal things were the vast concern. Here awakening and converting work was to be found in every part of the multitude; and even some things strangely and wonderfully new to me."

This phenomenon was intensified when a young Methodist minister named John McGee became so overwrought that he jumped up amid the benches of the congregation and began "shouting out the Devil." Like an epidemic, the fires of salvation spread through the crowd of "profane sinners and Sabbath breakers," steadily intensifying until not a dry eye or unbruised bone was left in the camp.

"The floor was covered with the slain in a moment and their screams for mercy pierced the heavens," is how one participant reported the experience.

The Great Revivals of the early 1800s, which raged through Kentucky and Tennessee like a forest fire, were born of these proceedings. So was the camp meeting, a marathon, multi-denominational outing that offered not only salvation to the masses but also an opportunity for people living isolated in scattered settlements to socialize.

Such outdoor meetings were necessary, since churches could not hold the throngs of people who converged on McGready's services. Volunteers built tents and lean-tos and long rows of split-log benches. They piled up wood for bonfires and built speaking platforms. Hoping, perhaps, to curry favor with God and McGready, many arrived early and competed with one another in the preparation of food and shelter.

Revival camps, frequently staged under the stimulating glow of the full moon, were often conducted on a round-the-clock basis, continuing for several days and nights. In many respects, they were the sporting events of their times, drawing tens of thousands of spectators and participants, who slept in improvised tents, in wagons or on the open ground.

Worshipers usually gathered as close as they could to the wooden platform where the prayer and hymn leaders presided. Sometime after the service began, the guest speaker, usually clad in a long black coat and hat, would appear on the platform, clutching the Bible. Silhouetted against the soft glow of crackling bonfires, the speaker would launch into his sermon.

The Great Revival reached its zenith during the summer of 1801 at Cane Ridge, Kentucky, when an estimated 25,000 people—one-tenth of the population of the entire state—descended on a camp to hear McGready and one of his converts, Barton Warren Stone, extrapolate on the Holy Word. Early in the service, according to one account, worshipers "abandoned themselves to frenetic bouts of falling, laughing, singing, barking and jerking as the meeting wore on."

These "exercises," as McGready called them, were necessary to reflect a "cleansing penitence by the sinner and divine approval by the Holy Spirit."

"The noise," wrote James B. Finley, a young Ohioan who partook of the service, was like "the roar of Niagara. ...The vast sea of human beings seemed to be agitated as if by a storm; I saw five hundred swept down in a moment as if a battery of guns had been opened upon them, and their shrieks and shouts rent the very heavens."

Finley added: "I counted seven ministers, all preaching at one time, some on stumps, others in wagons and one standing on a tree which had, in falling, lodged against another. ..."

The Reverend Moses Hoge wrote: "The careless fall down, cry out, tremble, and not infrequently are affected with convulsive twitchings. ... Nothing that imagination can paint, can make a stronger impression upon the mind, than one of those scenes. Sinners dropping down on every hand, shrieking, groaning, crying for mercy, convulsed; professors praying, agonizing, fainting, falling down in distress, for sinners or in raptures of joy!"

A Methodist named Jacob Young noted that many of the "smitten" gathered on their knees and barked and snapped "to tree the Devil." Finley saw some penitents bending spasmodically forward and backward, their heads nearly touching the ground at the end of each stroke.

Started by McGready and other Presbyterians, camp meetings became a characteristic feature of Methodist revivalism in the West, though they were never officially recognized by the Methodist Church conferences. Nevertheless, they helped to win thousands of converts to Methodism that by the second decade of the nineteenth century had overtaken Presbyterianism as the most dynamic of the frontier faiths.

But the revival ignited great quarrels among churches struggling to interpret the doctrines of Calvinism. Over the years, Presbyterians had believed in predestination—the belief that only God predestined a chosen few for salvation. Accordingly, there was nothing one could do to change one's state of grace. No amount of shouting, rolling or jerking could alter one's providential fate.

In the backwoods, however, far out among the lost and lonely souls of the wild frontier, unorthodox preachers like McGready veered recklessly from the church's teachings. They felt that sermons should be aimed at "the joints and marrow," rather than the mind, and that God would save members of the flock who did as his agents—the evangelists—commanded.

In time, however, McGready buckled under church pressure and ceased to preach his unorthodox views. After making "due submission" to tradition, he vanished forever from the public eye.

Joshua Abraham Norton

The Emperor of San Francisco

*W*hen gold was discovered in the California hills in 1849, thousands of starry-eyed adventurers flocked to San Francisco, each determined to cash in on the bonanza.

One of the most colorful characters to arrive on the scene was an ambitious, middle-aged merchant named Joshua Abraham Norton, who opened a general store and dabbled in real estate. By 1853, the intrepid businessman had piled up more than a quarter-million dollars and was looking to make more.

For some time he had watched the price of rice go up and up as supply dwindled, thanks in part to a Chinese embargo on the crop. Sensing that an even greater shortage was in the offing and that prices would continue to rise, the savvy entrepreneur sought to corner the market by buying up vast quantities of the commodity.

It worked—for a while. Then, when rice-laden ships from South America started steaming into port, the bottom fell out of the market. Norton, who had spent his entire fortune on this scheme, was ruined. Forced to sell his inventory at huge losses, he spiraled into bankruptcy two years later.

In 1857, still stunned and disoriented, the British-born businessman sank out of sight, eventually becoming a recluse. But not just any recluse. In a city saturated with eccentric losers and misfits, Joshua Abraham Norton would become the most celebrated of the breed.

Three years after his financial demise, the former prince of commerce emerged with a new identity and purpose. From now on he would be known throughout the land as Norton I, Emperor of the United States and Protector of Mexico.

To make sure his subjects got the word, Norton strolled into the office of the local newspaper and ordered that the following announcement be published on the front page: "At the peremptory request and desire of a large majority of citizens of these United States, I, Joshua Norton, declare and proclaim myself Emperor of these United States of America."

So began the storybook reign of Joshua Abraham Norton—or "Emperor Norton I," as he was known throughout his adopted kingdom. Overnight, Norton became a street celebrity—and one of San Francisco's most beloved characters.

Resplendent in secondhand officer's uniform with gold epaulets, beaver hat, tall boots and clanking old saber at his side, the emperor cut a dashing figure as he strutted about town, sometimes pedaling an old three-wheeled bicycle, issuing orders and proclamations at will. In September 1859, for example, he issued a decree that abolished Congress "because of corruption in high places." Henceforth, the cross-eyed emperor would rule in person.

When Washington ignored his decree, Emperor Norton ordered the commander in chief of the U.S. Army to "proceed with suitable force and clear the Halls of Congress." That was followed by another declaration aimed at putting down unrest in Mexico. Assuming the role of "Protector of Mexico," the emperor made it clear he would take an army across the border and restore order if the provincials in charge didn't put their affairs in order.

At the outbreak of the Civil War between North and South, the bearded old emperor summoned Abraham Lincoln and Jefferson Davis to a high-level summit in San Francisco. Neither man turned up, but more than a few San Franciscans were anxious to see how their proud leader would mediate an end to the bloody conflict. Later, the emperor graciously offered his allegiance and military support to Mr. Lincoln.

On other occasions, Norton "abolished" the Central Pacific Railroad, levied a twenty-five-cent tax on shopkeepers—which they cheerfully paid—and chided a police officer for once having arrested him on a vagrancy charge.

In many ways, Norton could not have picked a better place from which to rule over his dominion than San Francisco. As the center of the gold craze, the sprawling city by the bay was a bewildering melting pot of colorful thrill seekers and rugged individualists who seemed to relish their unconventional reputations. As such, they embraced Norton as one of their own, feeding him, clothing him—even providing their eccentric old friend with humble living quarters when he lost his house in the crash.

He rode the streetcars free of charge and traveled in complimentary train berths on his infrequent forays to cities in northern California. Whenever he entered a theater or restaurant, patrons would rise in respectful silence and salute. He even had three seats permanently reserved in the front row of the San Francisco opera house—one for him and one for each of his dogs.

A public referendum, initiated by the City Council, resulted in funds to keep him supplied with new uniforms as his old ones wore out.

In return for all the good deeds, the emperor saw to it that his was a kind and gentle reign. His loyal subjects were always treated fairly and equally, regardless of race, religion or social standing.

Twice a year he would review the police and fire departments as they paraded by, then make a grand speech to the assembled crowds. He printed his own money, which was accepted in business establishments around San Francisco as legal tender. When bicycles came out, San Franciscans got him a bicycle, too. When one of his dogs died, ten thousand people turned out for a "state" funeral.

Looking back, some San Franciscans argued that their old leader was ahead of his time. For example, he called upon other leaders of the world to join him in forming a "League of Nations" in which disputes between nations could be resolved peacefully. He also proposed that a suspension-span bridge be built across the spot where the Golden Gate now stands. He even laid out a complete design that looks remarkably similar to the bridge that was built sixty years after his death.

Many of the "decrees" attributed to Norton I were fakes, written, perhaps in jest, by newspaper editors for amusement or political purposes. Others, however, were the real thing, including one issued December 2, 1859, dismissing Governor Wise of Virginia for the hanging of John Brown and replacing him with John C. Breckenridge of Kentucky.

Another decree, issued July 16, 1860, dissolved the United States. On October 1 that same year he issued another proclamation barring Congress from meeting in Washington, D.C. Other decrees demanded that a worldwide Bible Convention be held in San Francisco and that the city of Sacramento clean its muddy streets and place gaslights on streets leading to the capitol.

Emperor Norton I "reigned" for four decades. On January 8, 1880, the beloved leader dropped dead on California Street at Grave Avenue while on his way to a lecture at the Academy of Natural Sciences. The next day, the *Morning Call* newspaper noted on the front page that "Norton the First, by the grace of God Emperor of the United States and Protector of Mexico, departed this life."

On January 10 he was buried at Masonic Cemetery with more than ten thousand mourners in attendance. The funeral cortege was two miles long. In 1934, Emperor Norton I was reburied in Woodlawn Cemetery by the citizens of San Francisco. A marble slab was placed on his grave with the simple inscription, "Norton I, Emperor of the United States and Protector of Mexico, Joshua Abraham Norton, 1819-1880."

In an editorial, the *San Francisco Bulletin* had this to say about the city's eccentric son: "The Emperor Norton killed nobody, robbed nobody and deprived nobody of his country—which is more than can be said for most fellows in his trade."

Gideon J. Pillow

Cowardly commander or misunderstood hero?

When the South needed a scapegoat at the end of the Civil War, one name stood out above the rest—Gideon J. Pillow, the blundering, cowardly commander who abandoned his troops in the face of battle at Fort Donelson and fled to safety.

Understandably, history has not been kind to this self-important lawyer-politician who rose to prominence before the war only to disgrace himself on the battlefield. Even today, Pillow's once proud name, a name linked with presidential campaigns and the power of politics of the mid-nineteenth century, remains synonymous with defeat, cowardice and treason.

"Pillow was one of the most reprehensible men ever to wear three stars and the wreath of a Confederate general," was one observer's telling assessment.

Ironically, only hours before the debacle at Donelson, Pillow vowed never to surrender his position. "And with God's help I mean to maintain it," he telegraphed his superiors in Nashville.

To understand the murky events that unfolded at the ill-fated Confederate fort, it is necessary to know something about the background of its flawed commander.

Born in 1806 in Williamson County, Tennessee, Pillow emerged early as a shrewd, successful planter and politically ambitious lawyer. Though he never held a high office, he delighted in undercover political manipulations and establishing relationships with friends in high places.

In 1844 he took full personal credit for the election of his friend, James K. Polk, to the presidency. Then, seven years later, he played a key role in the nomination of Franklin Pierce. In 1852 and again in 1857, he made his own bid for political office, seeking first the vice-presidency, then a seat in the senate.

He failed on both counts but became a powerful Southern spokesman for conciliation. After Abraham Lincoln took office, however, Pillow became a passionate secessionist.

Pillow's claim to notoriety was not based on his activities as a politician, but on his career as a vain, ambitious, quarrelsome and unsuccessful soldier. His gallant words, overzealous ways and penchant for self-promotion seemed to mask a complete lack of military know-how.

Fort Donelson, of course, constituted Pillow's most notorious failure. But there had been others, beginning with the Mexican War when he mistakenly ordered his men to build breastworks on the wrong side of a trench, leaving them completely exposed to enemy fire. On another occasion, he was censured by a military tribunal for quarreling with General Winfield S. Scott.

Pillow's courage in battle would once again be tested during the bloody battle at Murfreesboro in January 1863. According to eyewitness accounts, Pillow hid behind a tree rather than lead his men into the holocaust.

But it was the fiasco at Fort Donelson that cost him his command and ultimately led to his downfall. The record shows, however, that the beleaguered general had been on the verge of victory before Federal reinforcements threatened to overrun the fort and deprive the Confederates of their most important bastion on the Cumberland River.

Many Confederate diehards, unwilling to forgive Pillow for what they considered treasonous actions, went to their graves believing the "glorious cause" had been lost at Donelson. Although only 450 Rebels actually died defending the fort—relatively few compared to the carnage of later battles—the capitulation succeeded in opening the way south for the enemy and led to the fatal splitting of the Confederacy, which had been the Union objective all along.

General Albert Sidney Johnston, regional Southern commander and the hero at Shiloh, summed up the terrible price in a short message to a friend: "At 2 a.m. today Fort Donelson surrendered. We lost all."

Even considering Pillow's notorious track record, was it really fair to blame the loss of Donelson on one man? Or did it result from a breakdown in leadership involving several key commanders, notably John B. Floyd, Simon Bolivar Buckner and Nathan Bedford Forrest, all three newly arrived general officers?

It was Floyd, incidentally, formerly governor of Virginia and secretary of war under President Buchanan, who advised that the fort "would not last another twenty minutes" under Federal bombardment. He was the first to flee.

At first, Pillow wanted to stand and fight. Then he agreed with Floyd and Buckner that the fort was a trap and would cost them their army if they did not get out. Their pessimism had been bolstered by a somber pre-battle message from Johnston: "If you lose the fort, bring your troops to Nashville if possible."

Pillow's decision to abandon the fort followed a medley of mishap and misunderstanding that resulted in Donelson's eventual capitulation on February 16. Two days earlier, on February 14, Grant's navy had attempted to strike a blow at Donelson's water batteries but were chased away by high-powered Confederate cannon that sent most of the Union ironsides drifting out of control down the rain-swollen Cumberland.

At that point, hoping to clear the way for a breakout, Pillow ordered his men to attack Grant's ground troops. This they did with a vengeance, sending the superior Federal army reeling in surprise. Forrest's cavalry was especially effective, slashing through Union ranks like demons, leaving hundreds of enemy troops dead or dying in the freshly fallen snow.

The entire advance had been a success. Forrest wrote that the Confederates had rolled their opponents back for miles, "having opened three different roads by which we might have retired if the generals had...ordered the retreat of the army."

Then something strange happened. Rather than pressing their breakout, Pillow unaccountably commanded his weary troops back to the fort to rest and regroup.

Buckner protested, arguing that they must keep moving out in spite of exhaustion and disarray. He cautioned that the Confederates would be unable to resist a renewed ground assault by Grant's army.

Pillow balked, thinking he had won a great victory. He and Floyd telegraphed Johnston to inform him of their success against Grant.

By now Buckner was fuming. He knew the army's position was desperate and angrily told his two colleagues they should have marched out as planned while the way was open.

Now, with Grant's army closing in fast, it was too late. He voted to surrender. "It would be wrong," Buckner said, "to subject the army to a virtual massacre when no good would come from the sacrifice."

Pillow assented but advised his colleagues that it would be a Confederate "disaster" should he fall into Union hands. Floyd had the same high opinion of himself and concurred. His biggest fear was that the Federals would try him on old charges that, as United States secretary of war, he had made fraudulent deals and had treasonously shifted Federal arms to Southern arsenals where they could be seized by secessionists.

Around midnight Pillow called a command conference to debate final strategy. Senior officers attending the meeting included Pillow, Floyd, Buckner and Forrest. While Pillow suggested they either "cut" their way out or "make a fite," Buckner argued that the men were "too worn out and distressed" to make a stand.

Once again, Floyd and Pillow concluded that it would be a tactical error for either of them to become prisoners of war.

There followed one of the most bizarre changes of command ceremonies in military history as first Floyd, then Pillow, sought to shed responsibility for their troops. This remarkable event was dutifully recorded by one of Pillow's staff officers, Major Gus A. Henry Jr. General Floyd then spoke out, saying he would not surrender the command or himself. General Buckner remarked that if placed in command he would surrender the command and share its fate.

"General Floyd then said, 'General Buckner, if I place you in command, will you allow me to get out as much of my brigade as I can?'

"General Buckner replied, 'I will, provided you do so before the enemy receives my proposition for capitulation.'

"General Floyd then turned to General Pillow and said, 'I turn the command over, sir.'

"General Pillow replied promptly, 'I pass it.'

"General Buckner said, 'I assume it. Give me pen, ink and paper, and send for a bugler.'"

At that point, Forrest growled in disgust, "I did not come here for the purpose of surrendering my command," and stomped out. A few minutes later he led his entire regiment away without a single loss. Floyd and Pillow escaped by boat under cover of darkness. Buckner immediately sent word to Grant that he wished to discuss terms of surrender.

"No terms with traitors, by God!" Grant replied, then demanded "unconditional and immediate surrender."

Later, when Grant asked Buckner what had become of Pillow, the Confederate general replied: "Gone. He thought you'd rather get hold of him than any other man in the Southern Confederacy."

"Oh," said Grant, "if I had got him, I'd let him go again. He will do us more good commanding you fellows."

Pillow was eventually stripped of his command and brought up on charges of treason before a military court. George W. Randolph, the Confederate secretary of war, found him guilty of "grave errors of judgment in the military operations which resulted in the surrender of the army," but found no reason to question his courage and loyalty.

The humiliation endured by Pillow at his trial paled in comparison to the loss of his public image. He became, in the words of Nathaniel Hughes Jr. and Roy P. Stonesifer Jr., authors of *The Life & Wars of Gideon J. Pillow*, the scapegoat for "the myth, the grand excuse of Fort Donelson—that the Confederates could somehow have won the battle or escaped had it not been for Pillow's betrayal."

Critics continued to scream for Pillow's head, while legions of supporters hailed him as a "man of courage."

"Pillow is respected for his indomitable energy," a colleague wrote in 1861, "and for his unflinching bravery."

After the trial, Pillow performed admirably as director of the Southern conscription drive. During the final months of the war, he was placed in charge of Union prisoners.

For the rest of his life, Pillow protested bitterly the loss of his field command and against his "unfair" treatment by political enemies. In 1878, he died quietly in his sleep at his home in Helena, Arkansas.

William J. Simmons

"Under a blazing cross they will come"

On December 7, 1915, a hand-drawn ad appeared in the pages of the *Atlanta Journal* urging men of "intelligence and character" to join a new organization described as "The World's Greatest Secret, Social, Patriotic, Fraternal, Beneficiary Order."

The announcement, which ran next to a large display promotion for D.W. Griffith's immensely popular movie *The Birth of A Nation* was the brainchild of a fast-talking insurance huckster, self-proclaimed mystic and former circuit-riding preacher named William Joseph Simmons.

Only two weeks before, Simmons—who called himself "Colonel" Simmons because of his self-appointed rank in the New Order—had led a group of shivering followers to the windy top of Stone Mountain, Georgia, where they doused a crude wooden cross with kerosene, then set it on fire. While the flames hissed and crackled in the raw November wind, Simmons, a tall, red-haired man clad in a Prince Albert coat and a stiff-necked collar, raised his long arms heavenward and proudly proclaimed the rebirth of the Ku Klux Klan.

"Under a blazing, fiery torch," the colonel later proclaimed, "the Invisible Empire was called from its slumber of half a century to take up a new task and fulfill a new mission for humanity's good and to call back to mortal habitation the good angel of practical fraternity among men."

Thus was born the Klan, or at least the modern version of the semi-mystical society of hooded "nightriders" that flourished in the South during the Reconstruction era. Under the leadership of Colonel Simmons, the newly resurrected Klan, with its emphasis on symbolism, rituals and secrecy, would go on to become one of the most successful terrorist organizations of all time, appealing to large numbers of native-born white Protestants who feared their way of life was threatened by an erosion of Bible Belt values, corrupt politicians, and postwar immigration policies.

The reemergence and rapid spread of the Ku Klux Klan in the 1920s can in part be attributed to an earlier process of scholarly and popular cultural revisionism, which changed the way Americans viewed the post-Civil War Klan. According to the "tragic legend of Reconstruction" developed at the turn of the century by prominent Northern scholars such as William A. Dunning, John W. Burgess and John Ford Rhodes, rampant corruption and social disorder had characterized the years of radical rule in the South, with carpetbaggers, scalawags and semi-savage blacks viciously trampling on the rights of the native white population.

The legend of an imperiled Anglo-Saxon people valiantly struggling against the forces of barbarism and corruption conformed well with aggressive nationalistic and imperialistic sentiments that pervaded early-twentieth-century America; it also complemented emerging theories of inherent racial differences and black inferiority that an influential generation of sociologists and anthropologists were formulating.

Considering these overall trends, it was perhaps not too surprising that the Invisible Empire underwent a popular historical rehabilitation in the decade preceding World War I, most notably in Thomas Dixon's 1905 best-selling novel, *The Clansmen*, which portrayed KKK members as romantic saviors of the Old South. Within a decade, millions of proud, ruddy-cheeked recruits had swollen the ranks of Klan rosters, making the Invisible Empire a factor to be considered in the communal and political life of the nation from Maine to California.

But stories about the Klan's melodramatic rebirth differ. According to some sources, it was sparked by the success of Griffith's brilliant but racist film based on Dixon's book.

Colonel Simmons, however, went to his grave insisting the idea had been his all along, claiming that it had come to him in a recurring childhood vision. The visions, Simmons said, had been brought on by stories handed down to him by his Klansman father and an old Negro mammy named Aunt Viney.

"I was always fascinated by Klan stories," he said. "Aunt Viney and her husband used to tell us children about how the old Reconstruction Klansmen used to frighten the darkies."

The visions were always the same.

"On horseback in their white robes, they rode across the wall in front of me," Simmons once told a reporter. "As the picture faded out, I got down on my knees and swore that I would find a fraternal organization that would be a memorial to the Ku Klux Klan."

The Klan's founder was born in 1880 on a farm near the little central Alabama town of Harpersville. As a boy, Simmons dreamed of following in his father's footsteps and becoming a doctor. But financial reversals brought on by his father's untimely death forced young Simmons to abandon his dream and enlist in the army during the Spanish-American War.

After the war he became a preacher, riding the backwoods circuits in Alabama and Florida, where he developed his "fire and brimstone" oratory and eloquence, preaching on such topics as "red heads, dead heads and no heads," "women, weddings and wives," and "kinship, kourtship and kissing." His popular lectures defended traditional sexual morality against the forces of "ungodly modernism," a position his new Klan quickly embraced.

Later, as Imperial Wizard of the Klan, Simmons taught his followers to respect fellow Klansmen, reject the lure of sexual debauchery and refrain from carnal conduct with nonwhite women. He often compared himself to Jesus Christ, a prophet and victim living among devils and infidels. In this theocratic vision based largely on images of Victorian family life, Simmons would later picture Klan members as children, with himself—the Christ figure—as mother, not father. Symbols of womanhood and motherhood represented strength and constancy as well as racial vulnerability in Simmons' bizarre and rambling writings.

"I was the KKK's sole parent, author and founder," he once wrote. "It was MY creation—MY CHILD, if you please, MY first born, I, ALONE, am responsible for ITS borning and being. ... No devoted mother ever endured for her babe more mental anguish and gave more constant attention, through many sleepless nights and troubled days. ... Every dime I earned was earned to preserve its life and promote its development."

In 1912, after twelve years of preaching, Simmons was pushed out of the ministry because of inefficiency and moral impairment. For a while he tried his hand at selling female garters, then insurance. Unsuccessful at either, he soon found his calling in the attractive commercial field of fraternal organizing. Within two years, he boasted, he was out of debt and earning $15,000 a year as a district manager.

In addition to holding a top position with the Woodmen of the World, he belonged to several varieties of Masons and to the Knights Templar. He was post commander and a national aide-de-camp of the Spanish-American War Veterans, and was a member of perhaps half a score other organizations, including both the Congregational and Missionary Baptist churches. "I am a fraternist," he was to explain when anyone asked his profession.

During all this time he dreamed of founding his own fraternal order based on the Ku Klux Klan. When an automobile accident laid him up in bed for three months, he worked out all the details, then sat back to await the right moment to launch his new organization. That moment came in the fall of 1915 when T*he Birth of A Nation* was scheduled to be shown in Atlanta.

In its initial stages, the KKK was not a night-riding organization but merely a fraternal group that stressed "100 percent Americanism" and the supremacy of the Caucasian race. It was Protestant rather than anti-Catholic and favored "keeping Negroes in their place," rather than terrorizing them.

But when America entered World War I, Simmons and the Klan found a purpose and a role. The nation had to be defended against alien enemies, slackers, idlers, strike leaders and immoral women, lest victory be endangered. The Klan accepted the challenge. Robed followers of Simmons intervened in strikes, hunted draft dodgers, punished adulterers and occasionally marched in patriotic parades.

Whenever and wherever "100 percent Americanism" was challenged, Colonel Simmons and his hooded throngs with their flowing robes arose with pistols packed and loaded and crosses blazing. "Now let the Niggers, Catholics, Jews and all others who disdain my imperial wizardry come on!" he once told a Georgia audience.

The unsettled conditions of the post-Civil War South had fueled the rise of the first KKK, originally called the Kyklos (Greek for "circle") by its founders, a group of Confederate veterans who formed the organization as a secret social club in Pulaski, Tennessee, in 1866. Throughout the rest of the decade, as opposition to Federal Reconstruction policies intensified, Southerners seized upon the Klan as a promising agency with which to ensure the continued dominance of the Democratic Party and the white race.

Led by its founder, famed Confederate Cavalry General Nathan Bedford Forrest, this self-proclaimed "Invisible Empire" eventually spread to every former state of the Old Confederacy and inaugurated a program of terror against blacks and white Republicans, engaging in what has been described as "one of the most far-flung and persistent crime waves in American history."

The Klan's rituals, symbols and tactics—ghostly robes and hoods, midnight rides by torchlight, burning crosses—were singularly effective weapons against some untutored former slaves trying to adjust to freedom. Those who refused to be intimidated by these "spirits of the Confederate dead" were often tarred and feathered, flogged or lynched and had their homes burned.

By the early 1870s, pressure from federal authorities had driven most of the Klansmen out of business. Five decades later, under the direction of Colonel William J. Simmons, the hooded Knights of the Invisible Empire would ride forth once again, torchlights blazing, to spread terror and chaos. This time, however, the activities were not limited to the Old South; by the 1920s, local Klans had popped up in Pennsylvania, Ohio, Michigan and as far away as California. No longer was the Ku Klux Klan merely a regional phenomenon.

In Simmons' mind, nonwhite races in America should be sterilized to prevent them from diluting superior Anglo-Saxon blood. Never in the history of the world, Simmons preached, had a "mongrel civilization" survived. "What are the dangers which the white men see threatening to crush and overwhelm Anglo-Saxon civilization?" he asked rhetorically. "The dangers are in the tremendous influx of foreign immigration, tutored in alien dogmas and alien creeds, flowing in from all climes and slowly pushing the native-born white American population into the center of the country, there to be ultimately overwhelmed and smothered."

In spite of Simmons' impressive appearance, amiable personality and considerable talents as a public speaker, he remained basically a dreamer, a misty-eyed idealist who lacked real leadership and administrative talents. Perhaps realizing his limitations and yearning for continued growth, he looked for apostles to spread the gospel. They came in the persons of Edward Young Clarke and Mrs. Elizabeth Tyler, a pair of fund-raisers whose slick promotional skills and twentieth-century marketing techniques based on capitalist consumerism helped transform the Klan from a regional organization with a modest number of members into a powerful national force enlisting millions of eager followers.

By the summer of 1921, hundreds of thousands of Klansmen, many of them bored young men and women who turned to the Klan to escape the drabness of small-town life, had already paid their money and stepped across the mystic threshold to take their chances in the Invisible Empire. The nation was divided into regional sales districts, each headed by a district sales manager, the Grand Goblin. The various regions were further divided into state realms headed by King Kleagles, under whom the recruiters worked.

Usually the presence of a Klan in a town was announced by a Saturday night parade of hooded horsemen down Main Street, by a cross blazing on a nearby hillside or by a sudden appearance of Klansmen in the midst of a Sunday service. Robed in white and masked, they would march silently down church aisles, congregating before the pulpit to present a cash offering to the minister. Then they would read a Bible verse from the twelfth chapter of Romans, calling upon worshipers to present their bodies, through the Klan, as "a living sacrifice, holy, acceptable unto God."

At the core of the Klan was a belief system, engineered by Simmons, that held the organization together. Bound by a constitution that advocated "pure Americanism," the faithful pledged themselves to white supremacy and viewed with suspicion anyone who owed "allegiance of any nature or degree to any foreign government, nation, institution, sect, ruler, person, or people," and proudly asserted that Anglo-Saxons were "the only race that has ever proved its ability and supremacy and its determination to progress under any and all conditions and handicaps."

But all was not well within the hallowed walls of the Invisible Empire. Vicious quarreling, bitter disagreements over policy and frequent accusations that Simmons was an alcoholic, womanizer and financially inept finally forced the unrepentant old Imperial Wizard to resign in 1924.

Undaunted, Colonel Simmons spent his final days roaming the lobbies of Atlanta hotels reliving his long and bloody days of glory. He moved to Luverne, Alabama, shortly before his death in 1946.

Tecumseh

"We will all be Indians, united forever"

Chief Tecumseh never claimed he was a prophet or that he possessed magical powers strong enough to make the earth tremble and rivers flow backward.

But that didn't stop the strange stories being whispered about the great Shawnee leader around campfires up and down the Mississippi and as far north as the Great Lakes. Some followers said he could turn the sky black with a wave of his hand. Others said he had a special powder that could make his warriors invulnerable.

At least one tribe believed that Tecumseh, a tall, handsome ruler who quoted Shakespeare and predicted the future with equal ease, could make the trees of the forest fall simply by stamping his feet.

Meanwhile, as the legends about him spread, Tecumseh traveled among the far-flung tribes of the Old Northwest Territory, trying to persuade them to join an intertribal alliance to resist white advances. Everywhere he went, from Minnesota to Alabama, the message was the same: The white invaders could be stopped only by a strong confederation of tribes.

Tecumseh's "holy" mission would win him the hearts and minds of Indians everywhere but make him the number-one enemy of the emerging American nation.

"My heart is [like] a stone," Tecumseh remarked following the Treaty of Greenville on August 20, 1794, which gave the whites twenty-five-thousand square miles of former Indian territory in parts of modern-day Ohio and Indiana. "It is heavy with sadness for my people; cold with the knowledge that no treaty will keep whites out of our lands; hard with the determination to resist as long as I love and breathe. … Someday I will embrace our brother tribes and draw them into a bundle and together we will win our country back from the whites."

Born the son of an Ohio chief in the spring of 1768, Tecumseh had long been troubled by the increasing number of white settlers moving onto the land of his ancestors, driving off game and clearing sacred hunting grounds. Like many other Indians, he realized his people would soon be swallowed up unless they fought back.

In the spring of 1779, the situation grew so bad for the Shawnees that the nation split up, and hundreds of men, women and children left their homeland in Ohio and moved across the Mississippi, hoping to find peace there. Only a few brave warriors stayed behind to fight—including eleven-year-old Tecumseh and his family.

Four years later, in 1783, Tecumseh took part in his first battle against the whites. During that battle he killed four men—the most of any Shawnee warrior. Because of his courage and wisdom, he was made chief in 1788. Time and again the young chief led his band to victory. Soon his name had spread far and wide as a brave and noble leader who spoke with the spirits.

It is not known when the idea of banding the Indians into a vast confederation to drive the white invaders back occurred to Tecumseh. Apparently, he was still in his teens when he concluded that the only way to stem the surging tide of pale-faced outsiders was to obtain the cooperation of all Indians and to have them act in concert.

That was the message he preached to his people over and over as he sought to rally their support in what he called a "holy crusade" to block white advancement. By 1798, the charismatic chief found himself surrounded by a large number of adoring followers. One was his brother, Lowawluwaysica, a short, hot-tempered and somewhat deformed man who would become known as The Prophet.

That same year the Delawares, a tribe pushed out of lands given to them by treaty time and time again, came to him and asked for help. They had heard about Tecumseh, about his supernatural powers, and now they wished to join him in a mighty crusade to drive back the hated whites.

Within a year, impressed by the Shawnee leader's strength, vision and eloquence with which he held audiences spellbound, other tribes had come under Tecumseh's sphere of influence—the Potowatomies, the Hurons, Ottawas, Chippewas, Winnebagos, Foxes, Sacs and Wisconsin, to name only a few. He would speak with the Sioux,

Mandans, Cheyennes west of the Mississippi, and the Choctaw, Natchez, Creeks, Seminoles, Chickasaws and Cherokees in the South. He urged the Indians not to drink alcohol or to smoke marijuana so that whites could no longer take advantage of them during treaty negotiations. He also urged his followers to appear weak, to swallow their pride and fall back and wait. The time would come, he promised, when all Indians would rise up and fight together under his command.

And when that time came, Tecumseh told them, a sign would appear to all tribes on the same day and at the same hour and that all tribes, fighting together, would sweep across the land and destroy the whites down to the last man.

Tecumseh continued to travel, recruiting tribe after tribe to join his confederation and eliciting from them promises to commit their forces when the great sign was given. He thrilled his audiences by saying he would stamp his foot when the time came to go on the warpath and the earth would tremble and roar.

"Great trees will fall," he assured them, "and streams will change their courses, and lakes will be swallowed up into the earth."

The sign would "shake men everywhere to their bones like nothing they have ever known before." Indians would be expected to drop their hunting bows and hoes, to leave their fields and camps and assemble across the lake from the fort of Detroit. "On that day tribes will cease to exist," he said. "We will all be Indians, one people united forever for the good of all."

In 1805 Tecumseh and Lowawluwaysica, who now called himself the Shawnee Prophet, established a new village near Fort Greenville that was not a Shawnee village but an Indian village where all Indians, regardless of tribe or clan, were welcomed.

A year later, warned by Washington that they would be punished should they attack any white settlements, a group of warriors called upon Tecumseh and The Prophet for instructions. The frightened braves were told that, to prove their cause was just, the sky would soon turn black, and "night creatures will stir and the stars will shine."

When an eclipse appeared—right on schedule as predicted— Tecumseh's followers naturally attributed it to their great leader's command of the supernatural world.

In 1808, Tecumseh met with William Henry Harrison, the governor of the Indiana Territory, and promised him peace if the United States did not seize any more Indian lands through treaties. If they refused, Tecumseh threatened to unite his tribes with their British allies and make war on the Americans.

All along, Tecumseh had maintained that the Indians held the land in common with the Great Spirit, that no one tribe owned this or that territory. Harrison scoffed at the chief's suggestion, saying that if the Great Spirit had intended to make one nation of Indians he would have made it so they all spoke the same language.

Tensions continued to build along the frontier until 1811 when Harrison attacked Tecumseh's village at Tippecanoe. Harrison's mission was not only to annihilate the unsuspecting enemies but to capture Tecumseh and put him on trial.

As it happened, Tecumseh was away at the time of the attack. But his warriors, under the command of his brother, The Prophet, fought bravely, thinking their great leader had made the bullets of the whites harmless when fired against them.

At last, seeing that the fire of the whites was just as lethal as ever and that The Prophet had fled the battlefield, the demoralized Indians retreated. The Battle of Tippecanoe, which left sixty-one whites and an unknown number of Indians dead, dashed Tecumseh's hopes for an Indian confederation. Tecumseh was ruined.

But on December 16, 1811, the earth shook—just as he had predicted—when a strong earthquake rumbled across southern Canada and parts of the Ohio River Valley, forcing the Mississippi River to flow backward for a few moments. Trees fell, and huge boulders toppled, just as he had said they would. Lake Michigan and Lake Erie hissed and boiled as great waves broke on the shore. Farther west, the earth shuddered so fiercely that great herds of bison staggered to their feet and stampeded.

Many Indians who had deserted Tecumseh after the massacre at Tippecanoe returned and followed him into British service in the War of 1812. On October 5, 1813, Tecumseh—who had been commissioned a major general in the British army—was killed in battle, just as he had predicted.

The Indians lost perhaps their greatest leader ever, and the whites would go on to win the West.

Cyrus Read Teed

Tales from the hollow earth

*C*yrus Read Teed didn't set out to become the charismatic spiritual leader of one of the strangest religious cults in the late nineteenth century. Nor did this shy, well-mannered farm boy from upstate New York dream his name would someday be linked to one of pseudo-science's most bizarre theories: cellular cosmogony.

It all began during the Civil War when young Teed was called away to fight for his country in the Union army. During the war years, while recuperating from a sunstroke that left his left arm and leg paralyzed, he heard stories about strange creatures supposedly living at the earth's core. How was that possible, he wondered, unless the earth was hollow?

After the war he returned to New York and set up a medical practice specializing in herbal cures. He also started reading everything he could get his hands on about the mysterious realm inside the earth, leaving no stone unturned in his quest to learn all there was about the natural history of the earth as well as the cosmos. He read books, subscribed to newspapers and magazines, frequented libraries and attended lectures on the subject.

In time the knowledge-hungry young New Yorker found that many scientifically accepted theories circulating in those days clashed not only with his religious principles but with his own developing ideas of a smaller, more compact universe.

While working in his laboratory late one night in the autumn of 1869, Teed experienced what he called a "divine illumination." A vision told him how to turn lead into gold—an ancient alchemist secret known as the "Philosopher's Stone." Later that evening he had a vision in which God appeared to him in the form of a beautiful woman and revealed the secrets of the universe to him.

One secret that emerged dealt with "Cellular Cosmology"—the belief that the earth is practically stationary in time and space and exists as a concave sphere, with all life on its inner surface—kind of like a gigantic inverted cave. His controversial notion was outlined in a book called *The Cellular Cosmogony*, or *The Earth in a Concave Sphere*, which he wrote under his adopted name of Koresh, the ancient Hebrew name for Cyrus.

According to this view, the known world is located on the inside of the earth's curvature, beyond which there is only the darkness of a celestial void. At the center of the sphere, rotating in unison, are the sun, stars and other planets. The vast, internal cavity is filled with a dense atmosphere that screens the other side of the globe.

To prove his theory, Teed measured the curvature of the earth—a measurement that contradicted the Copernican hypothesis but which has yet to be disproved. In fact, he offered $10,000 to anyone who could prove wrong his measurements or theory. He found plenty of takers, but each time scientific measurements were made, the results were the same as Teed's.

More than anything else, Teed's belief in the concave earth was an article of faith, based on his own religiously inspired research and study.

"To know of the earth's concavity," he once wrote, "is to know God, while to believe in the earth's convexity is to deny Him and all His works. All that is opposed to Koreshanity is antiChrist."

The concept of a hollow earth was nothing new in Teed's time. Many people still accepted British astronomer Edmund Halley's theory of a hollow earth as fact. Halley, of comet fame, had proposed that the earth might consist of several concentric spheres placed inside one another in the manner of a Chinese box puzzle. More startling was the scientist's contention that some of these spheres might support life!

Famed adventure writer Edgar Rice Burroughs produced several novels with hollow earth themes. His fiction was preceded in 1864 by Jules Verne's classic study of life underground called *Journey to the Center of the Earth*. Both Burroughs and Verne had been inspired by the theories of an early-nineteenth-century American eccentric named John Cleves Symmes.

Like Halley, Symmes—an army captain and enthusiastic world traveler—believed the earth was made up of five concentric spheres, but suggested there might be a huge opening, known as Symmes Hole, at each of the poles. The ocean, said Symmes, flowed in and out of these openings.

In 1906, a book called *Phantom of the Poles* followed up on the hollow earth theory. Said author William Reed: "I am able to prove my theory that the earth is not only hollow, but suitable in its interior to sustain human life with as little discomfort as on its exterior. ..."

Somewhat more influential than Reed was Marshall B. Gardner, who rejected the "absurd" notion of Symmes but enthusiastically adopted the idea of openings at the poles. Gardner believed the interior of the earth was illuminated by a small sun about six hundred miles in diameter. When Admiral Richard E. Byrd flew over the North Pole in 1926 and saw no gaping holes, Gardner countered by suggesting the government was covering them up from the public.

Buoyed by these and his own findings, Teed decided he needed a quiet, isolated place to work and to establish his own concept of social and religious order. In 1894 he found such a place on the banks of the Estero River deep in southwest Florida—a three-hundred-acre tract of land he called the Koreshan Unity.

Starting with only a handful of followers, the evangelical alchemist and herbalist went to work building a new society dedicated to the principles advanced in his new cosmology. The new settlement—which he named Estero—soon opened its doors to scores of other disciples from as far away as Chicago. All along, Teed believed that Estero would become one of the world's great intellectual and religious centers.

In planning his "New Jerusalem" in Florida, Teed visited several communes, including one established by the Harmony Society in Economy, Pennsylvania. He saw firsthand the everyday workings of communal societies—models, he felt, of celibacy and communism. He also spent some time with the North Family of Shakers in Lebanon, New York, where he was admitted as a full member.

Teed and his faithful flock spent the next decade building more houses and libraries and churches in the wilderness. They also built a thriving tropical nursery, a handsome Art Hall, tennis courts, baseball fields, marinas, a general store and even a museum devoted to the display and interpretation of Teed's curious teachings and scientific research.

Teed eventually abandoned his herbal practice altogether and proclaimed himself the messiah of a new religion called Koreshanity. He launched a newspaper, *The Flaming Sword*, which helped spread his gospel until it ceased publication in 1949.

In spite of Teed's spellbinding oratorical and marketing skills, his "New Jerusalem" in the Florida sun never reached the population of ten million converts that had been his much-publicized goal. In 1908, two days after Christmas, the old visionary died from injuries received during a political brawl in Fort Myers, leaving behind his unfinished city and a personal and professional legacy steeped in mystery and legend.

To this day, no one knows where the enigmatic spiritual leader got the money to finance his project. Nor is it clear how he managed to lure scores of young women—many of them married—to his Florida hideaway.

After his death, Teed's body was placed in an immense mausoleum. The corpse was guarded twenty-four hours a day by teams of young women and men because of his promise to rise from the dead. Many of his followers believed he would be resurrected on Christmas Day the following year.

But in 1921, a hurricane struck the southwest Florida coast, washing away Teed's gleaming tomb along with many other buildings.

Forty years later the state of Florida turned what was left of Teed's religious and intellectual empire into the Koreshan State Historic Site.

Although the last of the original disciples died in 1981, site volunteers still offer guided tours and slide shows of the settlement. Many of the buildings erected by the Koreshans remain, thanks to rehabilitative and restoration efforts in recent years. Of special interest is the site's Museum and Library at the World's College of Life—Koreshan United Headquarters—on Corkscrew Road along U.S. Highway 41.

Here many of Teed's original books and furniture are on display, as well as an exhibit showing in three dimensions how his radical "cullular cell" theory puts the surface of the earth on the inside of the globe. Many of the founder's other bizarre beliefs are analyzed with charts and diagrams, including his contention that the moon is an illusion, that gravity is really centrifugal force and that a horizontal line on the earth's surface eventually intersects the earth's upward curvature.

Other displays seek to prove his theory that the sphere is about twenty-five thousand miles around, just as the scientists say, and that China is about eight thousand miles away, through the earth's center—straight up!

Nikola Tesla

Reclusive "crackpot" who changed the world

*O*ver the course of his long and checkered career, Nikola Tesla was called a lot of names—none very flattering. Some colleagues labeled him a crackpot, others a gifted madman. At least one contemporary accused him of being a carnival showman, while yet another suggested he was nothing but a medieval practitioner of black arts.

But when he died, more than two thousand people—including the mayor of New York City and the president of the United States—flocked to the Cathedral of St. John the Divine in Manhattan to pay tribute to one of the greatest inventive geniuses of all time.

No one would have been more surprised at all the hoopla than Tesla himself. A shy, reclusive electronics wizard whose bizarre style and unorthodox methodology had made him the laughing stock of the academic world, Tesla avoided publicity wherever possible, preferring the solitude of his lonely, fourth-floor laboratory on Fifth Avenue, just above Bleaker Street.

It was there, alone amid eerie glows and strange flashing lights, that Nikola Tesla discovered a dazzling new universe of electrons and light. Many of his ideas, such as alternating current (AC) motors, were years ahead of their time. Sadly, other scientists and inventors—including Thomas A. Edison, Tesla's life-long rival—often received credit for perfecting his proposals.

Only in recent years has this melancholy young scientist been accorded the credit he deserves. Among the bewildering array of scientific devices linked to his inventive brilliance are fluorescent lights, X-rays, the electron microscope, microwave transmission, satellite communications, solar energy, guided missiles, computers, the automobile speedometer, television, vertical-takeoff aircraft and radar.

Not bad for a Yugoslav-born immigrant who arrived in New York City in 1884 with a couple of his own poems and four cents in his pocket! Within two decades, however, the tall, stylish visionary with smoldering blue eyes and down-turned mustache had become the patron saint of modern electricity.

Tesla was born in Smijilan, Croatia, in 1856, the son of a clergyman and an inventive mother. He had an extraordinary memory, as indicated by his ability to speak six languages as a child. His mental abilities were so great, in fact, he was able to use creative visualization with an uncanny and practical intensity. In his autobiography he describes how he could visualize a particular apparatus, then actually test run the device, dissemble it and check for proper action and wear!

A graduate of the University of Prague and Graz Polytechnical Institute, Tesla worked for both Edison and George Westinghouse, but preferred independence in his own New York laboratory, where he enjoyed entertaining journalists and friends like Mark Twain with electrical "tricks." One of his favorite acts was to leap onto an electrified platform and remain motionless while millions of volts washed over his body, creating a kind of halo that surrounded him as he stood, suspended and unmoving, in his private universe of throbbing electrons and light.

Those who followed Tesla—and there were many—praised him for his contributions to science, which included the invention of the induction, synchronous and split-phase motors that helped bring hydroelectric power to Niagara Falls in 1895. His brain, wrote one admirer, was to the intelligence of other inventors "as the dome of Saint Peter's is to pepper-pots."

Few people doubted that Tesla possessed a brilliant mind; it was his personal idiosyncrasies that undermined his credibility and, in the end, brought him crashing to earth at the pinnacle of his career.

For example, the same man who foresaw plasma and gave the masses alternating current, invented wireless transmission, the cyclotron, robots and remote-controlled devices before the turn of the century, feared germs, compulsively computed the cubic contents of his meals and reacted with phobic horror to pearl earrings on women.

Small wonder that, when he died, one group of California disciples believed he was whisked back to Venus from whence he came!

As brilliant as Tesla was, so too was he chronically infirm and bedridden. As a boy, Tesla sought to cure some of his ailments by climbing up on top of a barn, breathing deeply, then leaping off with an umbrella billowing out over his head. While recovering from a nervous breakdown in Prague, he had a vision in which he saw the rotating magnetic field and alternating current induction motor he would later build.

The idea hit him "like a flash of lightning," he told a friend. "In an instant, the truth was revealed."

Using a stick, Tesla diagrammed in the dirt the wiring of an electrical motor. This drawing represented the rotating magnetic fields of an alternating current motor.

Tesla eventually went to work in Thomas Edison's laboratory, but the two temperamental, egocentric geniuses soon parted ways. They would remain rivals—some might say enemies—to the bitter end.

He eventually teamed up with George Westinghouse, who saw the practical advantages of the young immigrant's electrical inventions. For the rights to use his patents, Westinghouse paid Tesla $70,000 in cash and notes, plus a fabulous royalty of $2.50 per each horsepower produced.

Overnight, the brilliant but unknown young scientist was catapulted into fame and fortune. He lived at the Waldorf-Astoria and ate his meals at Delmonico's. Autograph seekers were a constant nuisance, as were women who constantly pursued the celibate loner.

One woman who fell in love with Tesla was Anne Morgan, the handsome daughter of financier J. Pierpont Morgan. They probably would have married had Anne not made the unforgivable mistake once of wearing pearl earrings on a date!

Tesla's feelings about women in general and marriage in particular were clearly revealed in a magazine article that appeared in 1897. Asked whether he believed marriage was suitable for persons of "artistic temperament," the brooding inventor replied: "For an artist, yes; for a writer, yes; but for an inventor, no."

In the same interview, he added: "I do not think you can name many great inventions that have been made by married men. It's a pity, too, for sometimes we feel so lonely."

By the turn of the century, Tesla's amazing career had started to decline. Some biographers have suggested it was due to a backlash from the academic community, perhaps jealous about his public grandstanding and the fact that he had never submitted a single article to an academic publication.

As a result, the legendary inventor soon found it difficult to arrange credit or to find backers for his studies. Where once major lending houses, industrial giants and the power brokers of Wall Street had rushed to his side for a piece of the action, Tesla now stood alone to face an uncertain future.

Near the end of his life, Tesla's bizarre behavior became even more pronounced. During electrical storms, he would have his black mohair sofa moved in front of a window. There he'd sit for hours, privately applauding the bolts of lightning with the rapture and relish of one artist appreciating the work of an equal.

He became a familiar figure in the park behind the New York Public Library where he fed the pigeons—"my sincere friends," as he called them. On more than one occasion he brought ailing or crippled birds back to his apartment and nursed them back to health.

In 1943, Tesla's rapidly deteriorating health resulted in a heart condition and constant fainting spells. Wishing to be left alone with his dreams and faded glory, he hung a "Do Not Disturb" sign on his door. The last person to see him alive was the hotel maid on January 5.

His body was discovered three days later on January 8. Nikola Tesla, the brilliant electronic wizard who changed the world, was dead at the age of eighty-six.

The day after his funeral, Tesla's huge laboratory on Long Island mysteriously burned down—but not before the FBI had rummaged through his files. No records were saved—and the remnants were bulldozed two days later. Such haste on the part of investigators led some historians to suspect that espionage might have been involved in the blaze. Could Washington—or possibly one of the Axis powers—have been looking for an experimental "Death Ray" weapon the great inventor was rumored to be working on?

It is worth noting that the motivation for the "Star Wars"

defense system of the 1980s was based upon fears that the Soviet Union had begun deployment of weapons based on high-energy principles developed by Tesla.

Tesla's contributions might best be summed up by a comment made once to a friend: "Let the future tell the truth and evaluate each one according to his work and accomplishments. ... The present is theirs, the future, for which I really worked, is mine."

Nat Turner

"I heard a loud voice in the heavens"

For years, Southern planters had been haunted by the specter of a massive slave uprising. On the dark night of August 22, 1831, their worst nightmare became reality when an axe-wielding band of blacks in Virginia went on a murderous rampage that resulted in the deaths of some sixty white men, women and children.

Led by a young mulatto and self-styled preacher named Nat Turner, the rebellion—the bloodiest in the pre-Civil War era—sent shock waves throughout the slumbering South, forcing many states to swiftly enact harsh new slave codes restricting movement of blacks. And as rumors of an even wider insurrection circulated among sleepy plantation communities from Richmond to Mobile, jittery whites locked their doors at night and went to bed with loaded pistols under their pillows.

In many ways, Nat Turner seemed an unlikely choice to lead the rebellion. Educated in the early 1800s by his masters, he worked hard, got along well with whites and was often called upon to help settle disputes among slaves. He even preached to a small congregation of slaves who were frequently joined by Turner's master, an illiterate but kind farmer named Joseph Travis.

But one day while working the fields Turner had a vision in which he saw "white spirits and black spirits engaged in battle, and blood flowing in streams." Only twenty-eight years old at the time, Turner interpreted the vision as a mystical revelation that he had been chosen by God to lead a holy war against the white power structure.

There had been other signs as well—voices inside his head, strange lights flickering in the woods late at night and, finally, a solar eclipse in the summer of 1831 that had been the deciding factor.

A charismatic speaker, Turner had little trouble rallying other slaves to his divine cause. Meeting secretly in the dead of night, Turner—who started openly calling himself "the Prophet"—quietly set about the grim task of organizing teams of killers whose duty was to "rise up and strike down the hated white serpent."

Some scholars say the idea for the rebellion was a fluke, that it had come to Turner spontaneously. Others suggest the bizarre plot had been festering inside him since early childhood. They base their belief on a legendary account about how his mother, reportedly a former African queen, had tried to kill him soon after he was born to spare him a life of slavery. She changed her mind, however, when a traditional search of his body revealed bumps and marks indicating he would become a divine prophet.

An incident in the early 1920s seemed to reinforce that belief. Hoping to reach Canada, Turner ran away from the plantation, eluding patrols for weeks. But a month later Turner chose to give up his own freedom and return to the plantation. Why? Some scholars believe it was because of his special status as a prophet.

Soon after he returned to the plantation, Turner married a slave girl named Cherry. After their second child was born, his owner fell on hard financial times and had to sell off his slaves. The Turner family was split up and sent to separate plantations. The angry young father turned to religion to vent his anger, and soon he was a popular preacher, visiting black and white churches in Southampton and Greensville counties on Sundays.

By all accounts, the young slave preacher was well liked by all, black and white. The blacks liked him because he was one of their own; the whites accepted him because he seemed to prove the value of Christianity in uplifting black heathens. He didn't drink, steal or gamble, was polite and worked like a mule during the week.

His most amazing religious feat occurred when he convinced a white man, E.T. Brantley, to quit as a slave owner and convert to Methodism. Turner even baptized the white man, a rare event in the antebellum South.

On May 12, 1828, Turner happened to be in the fields when a voice told him to seek the kingdom of heaven. He interpreted this to mean the end of slavery was at hand. These and other signs, including a full eclipse of the sun in February 1831, convinced him it was finally time to act.

Turner originally planned to strike on July 4, 1831. The rebellion was postponed at the last moment, however, when the Prophet became sick. "My mind was affected," he later explained. "The signs were not right."

But the signs were right on the night of August 22, 1831. Moving under cover of darkness, Turner rallied his followers and broke into his master's home first, slaughtering the entire family while they slept. From the Travis farm, Turner and about thirty followers armed with axes, old muskets, pitchforks and knives surged across the countryside, stopping off at every house and cabin along the way to stab, beat and shoot their white occupants to death.

The bloodiest carnage occurred at dawn the next day when Turner's gang of killers broke into the home of a widow getting her ten children off to school. The mother and nine of her children were massacred on the spot. The tenth child escaped by crawling inside a chimney where she hid until the murderers went away.

At every household the pattern was the same—terrorize the occupants, then kill them. There was no petty looting, no torture or rape, just killing. Only a few whites were spared, most of whom owned no slaves.

By eight o'clock, the enraged black rebels had hacked and bludgeoned their way across half the county and were now nearing the tiny town of Jerusalem. When the alarm sounded—sometime around nine—hundreds of militiamen charged after the renegade slaves, rifles and pistols blazing. Several blacks were killed outright, including dozens of other slaves who were vaguely suspected of complicity. Others, including Nat Turner, escaped into the Great Dismal Swamp.

Almost a month later the Prophet was apprehended by a team of marshals. On November 5 he was tried, found guilty and sentenced to be hanged. Throughout the ordeal, Turner remained calm and collected, unrepentant and seemingly unfazed by the angry demands for his life swirling across the jailhouse lawn. Some say the divine mystic and rebel leader actually looked forward to his date with the hangman.

A few days before his scheduled execution, Turner set forth his thoughts and feelings about the grisly deed during a series of interviews with his lawyer. What emerged were his so-called "confessions," a rambling, sometimes incoherent outpouring of love for his fellow man. Nowhere, however, did there appear any sign of remorse for the tragic loss of life he had caused.

Commenting on his earlier mystical experience that drove him to commit the bloody deed, Turner said, "I heard a loud noise in the Heavens, and the spirit instantly appeared to me and said the Serpent was loosed…and that we should…fight against the Serpent, for the time was fast approaching when the first would be last, and the last would be first. …"

Moments before the noose slipped around his neck, someone asked Turner whether he regretted what he had done. In a soft voice that crackled, the Prophet gazed down and replied, "I feel no guilt at all for what I've done. Was not Christ crucified?"

William Walker

The "gray-eyed man of destiny"

There was something strange about William Walker's eyes. One moment they could be soft and dreamy, the next wild and dangerous. Those who knew him often commented on the curious glow that came and went with his moods. Others said it was the color—that penetrating grayness that seemed to spill out from cavernous depths within.

"At times he could be quite godlike," remarked one biographer. "But it was the eyes—always the eyes—that carried the day for him. You couldn't escape the power of those steely gray pools."

According to an old legend among the Indians of Central America, such a man would one day walk among them—a liberator, a savior, a "gray-eyed man of destiny" who would usher in a new age of peace and plentitude.

William Walker believed he was that messiah, that man of destiny.

"I am not ashamed to say," he declared, "that I am favored by the gods."

In the beginning, the gods were indeed kind to this frail, bookish romantic who abandoned lucrative careers in medicine, law and journalism to pursue fame and fortune in the jungles of Mexico and Central America. Before his untimely end before a Nicaraguan firing squad at the age of thirty-six, Walker had become the darling of the American South, a folk hero to a generation of adventure-loving Americans, the "gray-eyed man of destiny" to his legions of followers.

Born in Nashville, Tennessee, in 1824, Walker fervently believed both in America's Manifest Destiny to dominate the continent and in the importance to the South of reestablishing slavery throughout Central America. He agreed with Commodore Matthew C. Perry's bold assertion that "Destiny...has doubtless decided that the vast continent of North America...shall in the course of time fall under the influence of Laws and institutions of the United States."

That conviction would drive Walker south to Mexico, later to Central America, where many Americans believed the enlightened forces of civilization were engaged in a natural struggle against barbarism. Clad in familiar melodramatic attire—a loose-fitting cape and broad-brimmed hat—Walker fancied himself a conqueror and prophet, an American Caesar.

After the war with Mexico in 1847, expansionist fever gripped the United States as restless freebooters and rugged soldiers of fortune known as filibusters sought by force of arms to seize countries and establish themselves as rulers. Walker had heard of such expeditions—and of the ignominious embarrassment and defeat of most.

But these forays, he reasoned, had not been led by men of his caliber. Where others had failed, he would succeed. Driven by wanderlust, embittered by the recent death of his fiancée, Walker became obsessed with the dream of conquest.

"The idea was simple enough," wrote biographer Roger Bruns. "Gather together the best available soldiers of fortune, equip them with weapons and supplies, rent a ship or two, sail to a Latin American country, usurp power, and become a dictator, president, king or whatever title of government or royalty one chose."

Fame and riches awaited the band bold enough—or ingenious enough—to prevail.

Walker, who stood five-feet-five and weighed less than 120 pounds, hardly seemed the godlike conqueror of his fantasy. With wispy blond hair, ill-matched clothing and shrill, quavering voice, there was little about him to suggest the quality of his toughness, his recklessness, his almost pathological desire for violence, action and adventure.

His adventurous career began in 1853 when he led a raiding party into the Mexican province of Baja California. After a series of successful skirmishes with local civilians, Walker proclaimed himself president of the new "Republic of Lower California."

Cheered on by the press, "President" Walker's next conquest lay just across the mountains to the east in Sonora—which he quickly annexed to his paper republic.

Within weeks, however, an uprising of angry Mexicans forced the foreign invader to flee for his life. Back home, newspapers and a growing number of supporters hailed the deposed president as a conquering hero.

Not so the United States government. Charged with violating the Neutrality Act, Walker was brought to trial in San Francisco. But he was acquitted by members of a sympathetic jury who saw in him the spirit of Manifest Destiny. In their eyes he was a courageous patriot and freedom fighter—a prime example of the rugged individualism that defined American character.

"Filibustering," wrote biographer Bruns, "brought the adulation and recognition he craved. Filibustering, he now realized, was his true calling."

Two years later, in 1855, the "gray-eyed man of destiny" led a private volunteer force into Nicaragua. The invasion—backed by Secretary of War Jefferson Davis—was a complete success. Now Walker found himself presiding over yet another regime—a regime into which he promised to introduce "the arts, science and agriculture; a government liberal in principle, committed to preserving peace and the vital interests of the nation. ..."

But the new president ruled with an iron hand. He plundered and killed. His men ran wild in the streets, raping and looting at will. His promised "democratic government in the true sense" soon dissolved into an orgy of hate, bloodshed and drunken tyranny.

Walker continued to dream of expanding beyond Nicaragua. His goal was to build a Central American federation and then attack Cuba—an idea warmly embraced by Southern slaveholders anxious to maintain political and economic parity with the North.

In 1856, thinking the decision would be politically popular, the president of the United States—Franklin Pierce—extended official diplomatic recognition to the Walker regime. By then, however, the once-triumphant filibuster had fallen on hard times. The natives had become restless, fed up with his empty promises of reform and his dictatorial ways. Without warning, they turned against him.

The biggest blow came when he alienated Cornelius Vanderbilt, the transportation magnate who had substantial business interests in Nicaragua. Jealous of "the Commodore's" vast holdings in his republic, Walker revoked the charter of Vanderbilt's Accessory Transit Company, a move that quickly backfired on the gringo president.

Vanderbilt responded by arming neighboring states in Central America. Their mission: oust the impudent invader from Nicaragua, the would-be king of all the Americas. So furious was the Commodore that his orders were to "drive Walker into the sea."

Soon Walker and his army of "Immortals"—so named because of their seeming invincibility—were on the run.

Walker returned to the United States a bitter man—convinced he had been betrayed. The regime of El Presidente Walker, it seemed, was at an end.

Invigorated by an adoring public, however, and a favorable press, the famed filibuster would return to Nicaragua in November 1857—and again in 1858. Both invasions failed, the second ending ingloriously on a coral reef near British Honduras where his ship went aground.

Still claiming to be the legitimate president of Nicaragua, the irrepressible invader defied a U.S. government order and headed for his adopted country once again in the spring of 1860. This time he attacked Honduras first—a move that sent British warships into action against him.

Forced to surrender to British authorities, he was turned over to Honduran officials. On September 12, 1860, the "gray-eyed man of destiny" was executed by a firing squad.

The death of this flamboyant filibuster, who symbolized for many slavery and the Southern way of life, sparked widespread mourning in Dixie, jubilation in the abolitionist North and a sense of relief in the war-torn states of Central America.

Sarah Winchester

Reluctant guardian of the spirits

$\mathscr{I}$f houses could talk, the rambling, multistory mansion built by Sarah Winchester in memory of her famous inventor-husband might speak volumes.

For almost four decades, the widow of manufacturer William Winchester, whose powerful repeating rifle tamed the Wild West, waged spiritual warfare against phantom invaders, spending millions of dollars to erect one of the strangest houses in the world—a sprawling, eight-story monstrosity of hidden stairways, trapdoors, fake roofs, upside-down pillars and sophisticated push-button intercoms that not even the men who installed them knew how to operate.

No expense was spared, as hundreds of architects, designers, carpenters and craftsmen—many of them working in relays—labored day and night for almost four decades to see the nightmarish project through. Upon its completion in 1922, the enigmatic structure boasted one hundred sixty rooms, three elevators, six kitchens, forty bedrooms, four hundred sixty-seven doors, ten thousand windows, forty-seven fireplaces, forty stairways, fifty-two skylights, seventeen chimneys, six safes and a single shower.

The bizarre building craze began in 1881, shortly after William's death when the melancholy woman received instructions from the spirit world to "go West." Afraid the spirits would harm her if she didn't obey, Mrs. Winchester moved to San Jose, California, where she bought an eight-room farmhouse owned by Dr. Robert Caldwell. Once settled in, the spirits again came to her during a séance, ordering her to enlarge the house—and to keep enlarging until further notice.

As long as the sound of saws and hammers filled the house, she was told, she would be safe from harm. As long as there was the clatter and clang of men at work, she could rest peacefully in her four-poster bed, knowing that she would live another day and that evil spirits would stay away another night.

Should the racket slack up—even for one moment—the spirits would return, legions of them, to taunt and torment the aged millionairess.

Hiring builders who worked shifts, Sarah commenced a lifetime project: designing a house and adding room upon room to it. The result was a hodgepodge of corridors and twisting staircases with many odd features. Some stairs led nowhere; fireplace pillars were installed upside down. Myth has it that she meant to confuse the spirits.

The elderly owner of the gloomy old house also had a strange obsession with the number thirteen—thirteen stairs, thirteen bathrooms and thirteen carpenters.

Mrs. Winchester's ordeal began innocently enough when she sought comfort in spiritualism to ease the despair she felt over the death of her infant daughter in 1875and the death of her husband, William, who succumbed fifteen years later from pulmonary tuberculosis. During a séance she was told that unless she spent all of her husband's money expanding and rebuilding the house, she would never know peace. Apparently, the souls of those killed by Winchester's rifles still held a grudge against him and were behind the unusual demand.

"Their souls...are restless," the medium calmly explained. "There are thousands of them...and they seek revenge." On a more cryptic note the medium added, "Your life will be cursed unless you buy a house, enlarge it, and continue building to it for the rest of your natural life."

As long as the cursed house was astir with construction activity, Mrs. Winchester was informed, she would not be troubled by the evil phantoms that dwelled in the closets and cupboards. Her instructions were to add on to the house constantly—to expand, renovate and rebuild, day after day, night after night—to fill the bulging confines of her huge old house with a cacophony of rasping saws and clattering hammers and groaning pulley systems.

She did as she was told, importing expensive doors, marble columns and priceless art-glass windows from Europe. In one room she installed four fireplaces and four hot-air radiators. In a climate where temperatures rarely come close to freezing, five separate central-heating systems were put into operation.

Through it all, the eccentric old woman kept a staff of eighteen to twenty domestic servants, ten to twenty-two carpenters and twelve to eighteen gardeners and field hands constantly busy. She followed no master plan for the house and, according to her carpenters, built whenever, wherever and however she pleased, always directed by the spirits. She built steadily, twenty-four hours a day for thirty-eight years, until her death in 1922.

"She had a good many spirits to appease so that when she was told by the psychic she should appease those spirits, it may have contributed to obsessive-compulsive behavior," says house guide Laurel Johnson. "The psychic apparently told her that if she was to appease those spirits, she should build a house and never complete the house."

In an attempt to drive out the evil spirits residing in cupboards and closets, Mrs. Winchester had them rebuilt into awkward shapes, sizes and positions. Eventually, two thousand cupboards were installed, some only one inch deep. To spare friendly spirits the embarrassment of not being able to see themselves in mirrors, Mrs. Winchester, upon her medium's advice, had only two mirrors placed in the entire house.

And since ghosts cast no shadow, the lighting of the rooms was arranged in such a way that humans couldn't cast shadows either!

For unknown reasons, several doors open only from one side, and others open into thin air. One set of stairs leads down to another set, then angles back up to the same story. Another peculiar stairway has forty-four steps and turns seven corners, but rises a mere nine feet. Yet another leads directly up to the ceiling with no exit!

Still not content with her grotesque creation, Mrs. Winchester ordered craftsmen to build a series of fake roofs and balconies to which there was no access. Pillars were placed upside down in several rooms. Miles and miles of wire ran throughout the house, connecting communicating devices that baffled even the installers.

Other architectural innovations and perversities abound—a

chimney that rises four stories only to end a few inches short of the roof; state-of-the-art fireplaces equipped with trapdoors for disposing ashes; inside cranks to open and close exterior shutters; a patented laundry sink equipped with a built-in soap holder and scrub board; and a clever system for collecting excess water from plants in her conservatory and delivering it to the garden.

Because construction had to continue without pause, Mrs. Winchester frequently demolished rooms or whole wings and had them rebuilt. Some rooms were walled off because of construction errors. According to one account, when she discovered a handprint in her wine cellar, she interpreted it as an ominous sign and had the room, with its contents still in place, sealed up.

Through it all, the occult-inspired homeowner surrounded herself with gangs of servants and butlers. Most were easy to hire, but, understandably, difficult to keep. As new chambers were added, the household staff found it increasingly difficult to find its way about the extravagant maze of twisting hallways, unusual stairways and oddly angled rooms.

"She had no master plan," one construction worker told a newspaper reporter. "She built whenever, wherever, and howsoever she pleased, always directed by the spirits."

In 1922, the spirit-cursed widow experienced chest pains but refused to accept the fact that she was dying. Instead, she ordered her laborers to work harder and faster, to make even more noise than before to keep at bay the evil spirits coming to claim her soul. Each evening she retired to her séance room to receive assurance and to get instructions for the next day's plans. As the work progressed, it became apparent the house was being constructed as much to keep in good spirits as to shut out evil ones.

Stories circulated that the old woman was so afraid of the spirits that she slept with rosary beads clutched to her chest and hundreds of lights burning throughout the house all night long. Maids were hired to keep her company constantly, never letting her out of their sight.

The pain in her chest gradually worsened. When the eighty-three-year-old woman finally died, the entire house fell silent for the first time in thirty-eight years. Workmen, genuinely saddened by their eccentric old employer's passing, laid down their tools out of respect.

For the next sixteen years, the old house remained empty. Not a creature stirred within—no housemaid, no carpenter, no evil spirit. Silence reigned supreme.

Eventually, permission was given to open the one-hundred-sixty-one-acre estate to the public as a museum.

To this day, however, some parts of the house have never been fully explored. Doorways and stairways lead to chambers yet unknown; entire wings remain undisturbed in the silently shifting shadows.

Not surprisingly, visitors and people working there have experienced strange phenomena—lights going on and off, rocking chairs rocking by themselves. One carpenter constantly felt a "cold breeze" when he walked into Mrs. Winchester's bedroom. Others noted a "tugging" at their collars.

Captain Henry Wirz

Monster or martyr?

*N*ot much is known about Henry Wirz, the ill-fated commander of the Confederate prison camp at Andersonville, Georgia, except that he was born in Switzerland in 1823, educated in Berlin, then immigrated to Kentucky sometime in 1849 at the age of twenty-six.

Those who knew Wirz described him as darkly handsome and intelligent, occasionally moody, but "always possessed of a kind and compassionate character." Critics called him a "monster" for his actions at Andersonville, while his legions of defenders in the Deep South hailed him as a patriot and martyr.

Historians say the truth probably lies somewhere in between.

"Whether Wirz was actually guilty of anything worse than bad temper and inefficiency remains controversial today," says James McPherson, author of *Battle Cry of Freedom*.

But when the war ended and the North needed a scapegoat for the purported sins of the South, "Heinrich" Wirz, the brooding, bearded commandant with the thick foreign accent, seemed the perfect candidate.

After his arrival in America, Wirz posed as a doctor, but it isn't clear whether he was ever certified to practice medicine. In 1854 he married a Mrs. Wolfe, a widow with two young daughters. The next year they moved from Kentucky to Louisiana, where another daughter, Cora, was born. When war broke out, Dr. Wirz was apparently enjoying a lucrative medical practice and was fluent in several languages, including German, Dutch and English.

After the attack at Fort Sumter, Wirz enlisted as a private in Company A, Fourth Battalion, Louisiana Volunteers. His regiment fought bravely at the Battle of Seven Pines in 1862, where Sergeant Henry Wirz was severely wounded in his right arm by a Minié ball.

Now useless, the arm proved to be a "source of physical suffering, right up to the moment the noose tightened around his neck," according to Ovid L. Hutch, author of *History of Andersonville.*

On June 12, after returning to his unit, Wirz was promoted to captain "for bravery on the field of battle." However, his wound rendered him unfit for battle, and he was detailed as acting adjutant general to General John H. Winder, the so-called "czar of martial law" and provost marshall in charge of Confederate prisoner-of-war camps. Shortly afterward, he was given command of two prisoner-of-war camps, first at Richmond in late August, then Tuscaloosa, Alabama, one month later.

Wirz's skills as a negotiator came to President Jefferson Davis' attention. In late 1863, Davis sent Wirz to Europe on a secret mission—to help Confederate diplomats gain the support of France and England. The following spring, Captain Wirz was ordered to the sleepy little southwest Georgia hamlet of Andersonville, where he was put in command of the newly constructed prison.

Andersonville, or Camp Sumter as it was known officially, was the largest of many Confederate prisons established during the Civil War. It was built in early 1864 after Confederate officials decided to move the large number of Federal prisoners in and around Richmond to a place of greater security and more abundant food. During the fourteen months it existed, more than forty-five thousand Union soldiers were confined there; of those, almost thirteen thousand died from disease, poor sanitation, malnutrition, overcrowding or exposure to the elements.

The first prisoners arrived in Andersonville in February 1864. During the next few months, approximately four hundred more arrived each day until, by the end of June, some twenty-six thousand men were confined in a prison area originally intended to hold only ten thousand. The largest number held at any one time was thirty-two thousand in August 1864.

Conditions became so cramped that one Union prisoner confided in his diary, "There is so much filth about the camp that it is terrible trying to live here. ...The air reeks of nastiness." Another soldier wrote: "Since the day I was born, I never saw such misery."

A young Georgia woman expressed fear of reprisals should the truth ever come out about Andersonville. "I am afraid," she wrote, "God will suffer some terrible retribution to fall upon us for letting such things happen. If the Yankees ever should come to South-West Georgia...and see the graves there, God have mercy on the land!"

If General Winder had not died of a heart attack in February 1865, it's probable the victorious Union would have hanged him instead of Wirz, and the doomed commandant's request to return to his native Switzerland might have been honored. In fact, before being whisked away in the dead of night to Washington, D.C., to face a military tribunal for war crimes, Wirz had been promised safe conduct out of the country.

But the North wanted blood. Sensational stories about the horrors of Andersonville had long circulated in the Yankee press. "There are scarcely words to describe the nightmare that is Andersonville prison," noted one observer. "Starvation, mistreatment, gangrene, maggots, dysentery, murder, unbearable stench— all inflicted intentionally by Confederate captors—seem sufficient to paint this ugly picture."

One graphic description of the camp's hospital, written by a doctor, appeared in a government report issued in September 1864: "The patients and attendants, near two-thousand in number, are crowded into this confined space and are but poorly supplied with old and ragged tents, and lie upon the ground, oftimes without even a blanket. No beds or straw appeared to have been furnished. ...

"I observed a large pile of corn bread, bones and filth of all kinds, thirty feet in diameter and several feet high, swarming with myriads of flies, in a vacant space near the pots used for cooking. Millions of flies swarmed over everything and covered the faces of the sleeping patients, and crawled down their open mouths, and deposited their maggots in the gangrenous wounds of the living, and in the mouths of the dead. ..."

At the trial, newspapers portrayed Wirz as a brute who took delight in torturing, maiming and killing Union prisoners. Headlines branded him "The Fiend of Andersonville." Public feeling was so strong against the Confederate captain that his own government of Switzerland declined to intervene on his behalf.

One prominent Washington law firm at first agreed to take his case, then backed off when it became clear its reputation would suffer.

The trial, which lasted four months, officially began on August 23, 1865, less than five months after the surrender of Lee at Appomattox. Two charges were leveled at the former keeper of Andersonville. The first claimed that he "maliciously, willfully and traitorously conspired…to impair and injure the health and destroy the lives of soldiers of war…in violation of the laws and customs of war."

In the second charge he was tried for the murder of thirteen prisoners. Three he supposedly shot to death with a revolver, while stamping to death another. Two more prisoners were said to have died while confined in stocks, another killed with chains and iron balls around their necks and feet, and yet another was torn to pieces by a pack of ferocious dogs unleashed on him by Wirz.

"He personally beat an unknown prisoner on the head with the revolver which caused the prisoner's death," the second charge read.

Witnesses, Union and Confederate, testified that the prison had been woefully overcrowded. Built to contain only ten thousand men, and later enlarged to accommodate another five thousand, more than twice that number were crowded inside the twenty-six-acre corral. Ex-prisoners and guards said there was no shelter from the elements "except such as the prisoners constructed themselves out of scrap lumber, pine boughs, clay, tenting or clothing."

"So the prisoners broiled in the sun and shivered in the rain," wrote McPherson.

Day after day, one shocking story after another emerged to seal the fate of the doomed commandant. It was revealed, for example, that prisoners often went without food and wood for days at a time. Even food served to them was uncooked and infested with blight and bugs. A small, garbage- and waste-filled creek that trickled through the center of the camp provided inmates with their only source of water.

Witnesses also testified that open sinks set aside as privies became so clogged with human waste that the stench was carried by prevailing winds for several miles around.

Ironically, of the one hundred forty-five witnesses called to the stand, only fifteen had anything negative to say about Wirz personally. Father Peter Whelan, the Catholic priest who had ministered to prisoners at Andersonville, said he never saw or heard of Wirz murdering a prisoner. One former Federal prisoner, Frederick Giuscetti of the 47th New York Regiment, swore he had always been treated "in the kindest manner" by Wirz.

So compelled was he to defend the beleaguered ex-commandant, Giuscetti sent a letter to *The New York Times* asking readers desirous of a fair trial for Wirz to send financial contributions to the Swiss Consul General in Washington. He also called for other former prisoners of war to come forward and speak out on Wirz's behalf.

But the North needed someone to blame for the horrors at Andersonville. Not surprisingly, the court found Wirz guilty and sentenced him to hang. On November 10, 1865, amid cries of "Remember Andersonville!" by Union soldiers in attendance, the prisoner was led to the gallows in the yard of Washington's Old Capital Prison. Before slipping the black hood over the prisoner's head, the officer in charge, Major George B. Russell, asked Wirz if he had any last words.

"I have nothing to say to the public," Wirz replied. "But to you I say I am innocent. I can die but once. I have hope for the future."

A few weeks earlier he had written a final appeal to President Andrew Johnson protesting his innocence. "For six weary months I have been a prisoner," he said. "For six months my name has been in the mouth of every one; by thousands I am considered a monster of cruelty, a wretch that ought not to pollute the earth any longer. ... But, oh, sir, while I wring my hands in mute and hopeless despair, there speaks a small but unmistakable voice within me that says: 'Console thyself, thou knowest thy innocence.' "

He concluded: "The pangs of death are short, and therefore I humbly pray that you will pass your sentence without delay. Give me death or liberty. The one I do not fear; the other I crave. If you believe me guilty of the terrible charges that have been heaped upon me, deliver me to the executioner. If not guilty, in your estimation, restore me to liberty and life."

Wirz understood that his pardon request would be denied. In a final note, he asked only that his family be provided for.

On the gallows, the doomed officer shook hands with Major Russell. "Thank you for your courteous treatment, sir," he said softly.

Russell then draped the hood over the head of the doomed man. Another thunderous roar of cheers rolled over the crowd when Russell lifted his cap and the trapdoor sprang open beneath Wirz's manacled feet, leaving him dangling at the end of the rope.

According to Russell, Wirz's body jerked in spasms for seven full minutes. Doctors waited until nightfall before removing the corpse, which was then buried in the arsenal yard near the graves of the Lincoln conspirators.

In 1869 Wirz was reinterred in Mount Olivet Catholic Cemetery in Washington, his grave marked by a small, simple stone reading "Wirz." In 1960, a companion stone, placed there by an anonymous sympathizer from South Carolina, was added. It reads: "Captain, C.S.A. Martyr."

A monument in Wirz's memory at Andersonville bears the text of Jefferson Davis: "When time shall have softened passion and preju-dice, when Reason shall have stripped the mask from representation, then Justice, holding evenly her scales, will require much of the past censure and praise to change places!"

Was forgiveness possible? Considering the post-war climate, that seemed highly unlikely. Walt Whitman summed up the North's feelings when he wrote: "There are deeds, crimes that may be for-given but this is not among them. It steeps its perpetrators in blackest, escapeless, endless damnation."

Yet controversy over the justice of Wirz's execution continues. In an article published in 1890, Jefferson Davis exonerated Captain Wirz, saying, "He died a martyr to a cause through adherence to truth."

The late historian Bruce Catton, hardly a Confederate sympa-thizer, wrote in 1959 that "Wirz was a scapegoat, dying for the sins of many people, of whom some lived south of the Potomac River, while others lived north of it."

Wovoka

Mystic warrior of the Plains

*O*n New Year's Day in 1889, a young Paiute Indian mystic named Wovoka had a dream. In that dream he died and went to heaven where God commanded him to take a message back to earth. Wovoka was to tell Indians everywhere that if they would follow God's commandments and perform a "Ghost Dance" at regular intervals, their old days of happiness and prosperity would return.

"All the people of the earth will be swallowed up," the Great Spirit told him, "but at the end of three days, the Indians will be resurrected in the flesh to live forever. Once again there will be plenty of game, fish and pinion nuts."

Best of all, the white invaders would be destroyed forever.

Wovoka's dream sounded good to weary warriors who yearned for the good old days before the coming of the white man. During the decade following the defeat of General George Armstrong Custer and his Seventh Cavalry at the Little Big Horn, Western tribes had steadily lost power, then been driven onto reservations.

Most of the great chiefs and mighty warriors were dead. The buffalo and antelope had almost vanished. The old ceremonies of the tribes had become rituals without meaning.

Wovoka's new religion held forth a vision of paradise in which all Indians would at last be free of the white burden and reside for eternity in a blissful land. In the words of Robert Utley, author of *The Indian Frontier*, it would be "a land without white people, a land inhabited by all the generations of Indians that had gone before, a land bounteous in game and all the other riches of the natural world, a land free of sickness and want, a land where all peoples dwelt in peace and with one another."

All Indians who danced the Ghost Dance would be taken up into the air and suspended there while the new earth was being laid down. Then they would return to earth, along with the ghosts of their ancestors. Only Indians would live there then. In January 1889, the first so-called Ghost Dance was performed at Walker Lake Reservation. The dancing continued for a day and a night, Wovoka sitting in the middle of a circle before a large fire with his head bowed, muttering a low chant. Shirts with magic symbols painted on them were passed out to the participants. Those who wore the shirts, explained Wovoka, would be shielded from harm. On the second day he stopped the dancing and described the visions that God had sent to him. Then the dancing commenced again and lasted for three more days.

Wovoka called his religion the Ghost Dance because it preached that all the ghosts of dead Indians were waiting to return to help living Indians in their hour of need. From this, a great revival spread among the emotional people of the Plains, and within weeks the Utes, Bannocks, Cheyenne, Shoshone and Sioux were following the Paiute messiah, hopeful that he would lead them all back to their days of glory.

The Sioux accepted the Ghost Dance religion with more fervor than any other tribe. Wovoka, they believed, was the true messiah. Some who had seen him preach said he had descended from heaven in a cloud.

The fact is, Wovoka was born about 1856 in Esmeraldo County, Nevada, believed to be either the son or nephew of an eccentric old Paiute visionary named Tavibo. As a boy growing up in an isolated valley of sage prairie and surrounded by ice-crowned sierras, young Wovoka developed early an appreciation for the supernatural world of his father. It was Tavibo who had spearheaded a religious movement among Great Basin tribes, a movement that included dancing in circles and chanting.

During his early twenties Wovoka went to work for a white rancher named David Wilson. It was during this time that Wovoka, nicknamed Jack Wilson by his boss, learned to read English and developed a keen interest in Western theology.

On January 1, 1889, Wovoka witnessed a solar eclipse while in a trance. Out of this "spiritual awakening," as he called the experi-

LECTURES & BOOKS

E. RANDALL FLOYD offers lectures on a number of topics, ranging from strange and unusual aspects of Civil War history to the paranormal. If you want to contact Mr. Floyd to arrange lectures, guest appearances or autograph signings, please call the Augusta office at 706-738-1308 or 706-738-0354, or write Harbor House, 3010 Stratford Drive, Augusta, Georgia 30909, for further information. Or you may e-mail him at harborbook@aol.com.

A SURVEY OF METAPHYSICS